The Prophecy Map of Nova Gaia

The Cartographers of the New World

THE PROPHECY MAP OF NOVA GAIA

novagaialove.com

To contact the publisher:
waychilllife@gmail.com

First edition

ISBN: 9798578026836

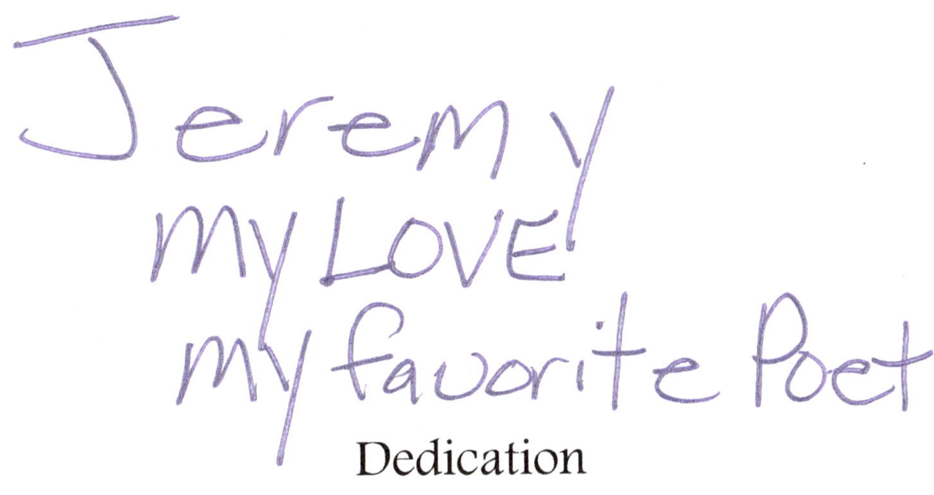

Dedication

To All the Seekers of the New World

May the love of the NOW always BE now
Rachel O
Dragon Heart

Acknowledgements

We acknowledge you.
We acknowledge your struggles, your pain,
your triumphs, your spiritual work.
We acknowledge your confusion over the changes
that have been taking place around the world.
We acknowledge and honor you
for the path you have chosen in this lifetime.

Table of Contents

A Future of
Love,
Forgiveness,
and Compassion
was Foreseen.

Our Beginning

On a rainy day in April in the global pandemic year of 2020, three women came together in virtual space to discuss Love, the energies of the Earth, and how best to nurture the future.

A future of Love, Forgiveness, and Compassion was foreseen.

A time and place where competitive values of war, hierarchy, and competition fade impotently away, individually and collectively, finally out growing old outworn childhood tantrums.

A time and place where humanity overcomes traumas and the fight or flight panic of living constantly in survival mode.

A time and place where each individual and each collective claim their birthright to thrive, taking this Compassion, this kindness, this Love and this growth to heart and into action.

While each of these women was living in her human form, each individual woman also carried her own unique energy signature. These miraculous energies came together, The Fairie, The Angel, and The Dragon Heart, to midwife the birth of a New World.

One thing these three women immediately recognized was the failure of the old world energy to bring true peace and healing to its inhabitants. In keeping its focus on the thorn, the old world energy had failed to know the rose.

The old world energy could not grasp the tenderness, could not fully hold the all-encompassing Love and beauty of the world of the Divine.

While many seekers had fought valiantly to bring peace and healing to Earth, the dominant energy of the now-fading world worked frantically to deny humanitarian values and ignore the Divine. More than that, the dominant power of the old world energy worked in many subtle ways to denigrate and abuse all that was beautiful and pure so the world would stay in ignorance.

We were grateful to those who paved the way for us to learn, to expand, and to thrive, yet many past teachers and gurus seemed unable to lift their teachings out of the old energies of competition, division, hierarchy, legality, and dogmatic structure. In the new world of Nova Gaia we come to fully express the values of cooperation, equality, togetherness, transparency, and freedom not only in words but in every action of our living beings.

It was difficult to know which of the three women first spoke her truth aloud, since the feelings expressed simultaneously danced at the edges of their lips, demanding to be said. These women – this Angel, this Dragon Heart, this Fairie – were tired of being silenced by others who put themselves forward as gurus and leaders of the new while so obviously keeping their tactics and attitudes firmly stuck in the energy of the old.

"So much ego and name-dropping!"

"The constant conspiracy theories and war rhetoric!"

"They just don't get it."

"They call themselves representatives of the Divine Feminine! It doesn't ring true. Where are the true voices of the new energies? I want to hear women's voices and teachers who truly embody the Divine Feminine!"

Yes, the three women wondered, where were the new leaders for this new world?

Many older leaders, true-heart leaders, had taken great strides forward to get the world to its current place, but the time had come for new leaders, for new voices. The hearts of these three women told them that these shining new leaders were out there, somewhere. They could hear them, not with their ears, but with their hearts.

These new leaders were quiet, humble, and only heard in the rare moments of silence that exist between the loud cannon-like words of the outworn ego-based energies. Many humans were hearing the call, coming into their own as leaders who no longer had to emulate the old model of success in order to be valued as the Pathfinders and Wayshowers they were born to be.

Then they heard it. These three women heard it. The Clarion Call to step forward and serve sounded in the space around them and its message was clear.

These three women are here to collaborate, to raise and support one another as they go forward to explore these new energies, these new ways. They are to discern new pathways, new ways to walk softly with the Mother, Gaia. They are to lift their voices to share their discoveries with others.

They are Cartographers of the New World.

The Dragon Heart, whose knowledge reaches back to the moment when time began, was prepared to get the messages out. She had seen hints of this moment coming over the past years and had prepared the structure to support it. The Dragon Heart knew the importance of reaching people. She was ready to create events, ready to reach out with blogs, podcasts, seminars, retreats, and a shining Love Expo.

The Angel, who knew the peace and beauty of Heaven and was often hurt by the sorrows of this world, knew the power of the Word. She wanted so desperately for this world to become the highest and best version of itself. She was ready to use the Word to take possibilities and pull them into existence.

The Fairie, a delightful blend of this world and other worlds, smiled at her friends with a knowing smile. She had been learning about the science of this world and expanding her comprehension of the metaphysical world. She was ready to be the bridge from the heart of Spirit to the hearts of humans.

Coming together, these three women all knew that the never-before-experienced level of Love energy that now encircled the Earth was the key, or more appropriately the Qi. Increasing the amount of this new level of Love in the cumulative vibration of all things would open lock after lock after lock, opening doors to increased compassion and kindness.

The Fairie, The Angel and The Dragon Heart knew that Love was the only energy that mattered, the only energy that could birth the transformation that was coming – for it *would* come. Many humans around the world and many beings across the Universe would experience the ascendency of Divine Love on Earth.

The Dragon Heart, The Angel, and The Fairie – each one had been raising the vibration of her heart for years, expanding the capacity of her heartspace to hold and express Love energy fully and completely.

How to go forward they didn't yet know, but they trusted Spirit to lead the way.

Maps. They would create maps with words, with events, with classes. They would support these maps with blogs, with podcasts, with social media, and with the energy that flowed from them like colors from a rainbow. Whether their maps reached many or only a few didn't matter. They knew their maps would be discovered by the treasure seekers who were ready to set avarice aside and reach for the only real treasure there is: The treasure of forgiveness. The treasure of compassion. The treasure of Love for All.

You, my friend, are that treasure seeker. You hold in your hand the first map for a new world.

We are The Cartographers of the New World.

A Message from The Angel

A few years ago I received a series of extraordinary intuitive messages with a unique and different energy as I gave reiki sessions. I had been receiving intuitive messages during reiki sessions for years, but these were different, somehow. More profound. These were important in a way I couldn't yet fully understand.

These messages weren't just for me and my clients on the reiki table. These were teachings for the world. These messages were for *you*. These teachings were for *now*.

I was guided to write down these messages from Spirit, documenting this remarkable time. When this intensely rewarding period came to its natural close, I sat down to compile all of these written messages together for a book. As I started to type I heard clearly, "This is not the right time. This is not the right book."

Over the years I have learned to trust, learned to release, and learned to value myself without concern for accomplishments, so I listened and waited. Perhaps these messages had served their purpose and there was no further task for me. So I let them go. I gave thanks for the part I had played and the lessons I had learned, and I released all attachment to the messages I had collected. Ultimately, I forgot about the file of session notes on my computer.

When I joined with The Dragon Heart and The Fairie and we discovered our combined destiny as the Cartographers of the New World, a new light was lit inside each of us. Immediately we began to work on our Maps of Nova Gaia.

Out of the blue, Spirit reminded me of the intense reiki session messages I had received two years prior.

When I shared these incredible teachings with The Fairie and The Dragon Heart it was no surprise to find that they, too, had received significant messages of a similar nature, preparing them for this moment. These teachings are now demanding to be shared with the broader world so these special energies and lessons can be integrated and learned by all.

It is the right time.

These prophetic messages could not be shared earlier. It wasn't yet time. They were not for the old energies of the old world. These prophetic teachings are part of the Nova Gaia energies and Nova Gaia experience.

We, the Cartographers of the New World, were given these messages in preparation for this moment. This perfect moment when you and I and The Fairie and The Dragon Heart and these pages come together.

Spirit has a message for you:

This is the right book.

Entering Nova Gaia

Energetically speaking, we are starting life in a whole new world. This is known as The Shift, or you may have heard it called Ascension. It sounds like something most people would expect to find in a science fiction novel, only this time it is real. Energy isn't just the power that charges your cell phone. It is something that is all around us, in us, and through us. Many people who are sensitive to energy have felt the density of the old Earth energy pushing us down, holding us back.

With the new energies of Nova Gaia we are now able to experience a lighter, finer energy; one that holds the promise of something kinder. Everything IS Energy. What you are feeling now are higher frequencies that are integrating.

Initially this lighter energy may not make you feel happy and loved. Your initial reaction may be annoyance because the contrast of this perfectly complete and abundant energy makes you aware of how much better we *could* do as human beings.

It can no longer be said that we of Earth must accept the past darkness and density of our planet and our societies because "that's the way it's always been and you can't do anything about it." We can all experience something brighter, something filled with the essence of Love and respect and honor and joy and health and abundance. True oneness is possible. This has been foretold. True oneness is inevitable.

Divine Energy, by whatever name you prefer to use (God, Goddess, Spirit, Source, The Creator, All That Is, *ALL*, etc.) has been bringing us to this point in time and energy. Spirit has been steadily raising the energies of Earth and all her inhabitants. The typical terms used by humans are "raising the vibration" of Earth, or "shifting from the 3rd Dimension to the 5th Dimension". Some use even higher designations such as 8D (the 8th Dimension) or 12D (the 12th Dimension). In essence, we are leveling up. All of us.

It really doesn't matter what number you use. The numbers are just there to help with our human understanding. The spiritual world doesn't need numbers or levels. The world of Spirit isn't concerned with the kind of hierarchy numbers imply. It is just a matter of different frequencies.

4D is the step where we are being prepared to enter 5D and beyond. When we each decide to leave 3D behind in a conscious way, 4D tackles the actual cleansing of our personal energies so when we enter 5D much of our low frequency energies have been completely cleared.

We humans of the current age are true multitaskers. Beginning in the year 2012 and continuing for a number of years, most of humanity went through 4D as part of an immense transition. It is that time of personal isolation you experienced in your life, your "dark night of the soul" that lasted for many, many nights and days. Many of those who avoided this experience had it thrust upon them in the form of the worldwide pandemic of 2020 with enforced isolation. 4D is our transition, our platform to step up.

Getting to 5D and beyond isn't easy. This can be especially true for those individuals who have no idea that they possess an energy body. When a big energy upgrade comes along, the only thing these people know is that they feel horribly uncomfortable for no reason at all. When a person is aware of the energy changes and has the tools to navigate them, it becomes easier.

With experience, you learn how to surf the energy waves. You learn to be gentle with yourself. When you accept and allow these new Nova Gaia energies for yourself, the Highest Good happens for you and for the Greatest Good of All.

Since our Earth, Gaia, has entered 5D, all of her inhabitants have to follow. Nova Gaia will not allow lower energies to enter her any longer. Just look at the children and see how wise they are; they know this.

Those of us who are not born into the new energies have to do our cleanup and it is not always pretty. We do have a compass in each of us. This compass gets stronger each year as there is more light within the energy of all that is Gaia, including us. That compass gives a clear direction about what is the right thing to do. The younger you are, the less you can ignore that compass.

When I, The Fairie, was born into a human body in the 1950s, the world was quite a dark, dense place. In order to ground and be present on this planet I had to leave a lot of my original blueprint and wisdom in the higher dimensions and forget who I was. The human template then could only hold so much information (think memory, the hard drive of a computer).

Every year since, and especially since 1987, the year of the Harmonic Convergence (the year I moved to California) the energy got lighter and brighter. Human energy now can hold more light/information and does not have to forget so much of their original blueprint to find grounding on this Earth. Every year, the babies born forget less of who they are and where they came from (Spirit).

These babies have innate wisdom that they can bring from the very beginning into the human experience and have much more balanced knowing about self. They are also raised into an old system that is on its last breath that brings confusion and "wanting to fit in" when they know they do not. Most of us have grown up never fitting in, either. I can relate to the deep insecurity that this confusion brings. But with each year, the babies bring more of their higher self into the human body.

In this process, as our body changes from carbon based to crystalline, we can hold more information. I know from my own personal experience how grateful these kids and young adults are when they finally hear that what they are feeling inside holds a deeper truth. That it is not them, but the world, society, that is messed up; when they are allowed to feel the truth that their sense of what is right and what not is spot on.

There are many incredible people all around the globe who chose to incarnate at this time specifically to help birth this new world, this Nova Gaia. These Lightworkers are here to bring in and modify these new energies, making the energy easier to digest for the unawakened bulk of humanity.

If you are reading this, you are probably one of these amazing volunteers. You are a Lightworker. You have likely been hit hard by the energies because you are not just transmuting them for yourself – that would have been very easy for you with your special capabilities. You have been transmuting energies for the benefit of everyone and everything on this planet.

Bit by bit, over a period of many years, the energies in and of the Earth have been rising higher and higher. This has occured slowly, allowing us to adjust to them. A sudden move from 3D to 5D would completely destroy humankind. While holding the lower vibrations of the old world, our bodies and minds would not be capable of handling the shift.

This is known because it has already happened before. Yes, humanity has grown and evolved and been destroyed in the process a number of times before. According to Indigenous knowledge and ancient mythical information, we are entering the 6th world. Five worlds have failed before, including Atlantis, Noah's Flood and Lumeria.

This time, we are being shown and guided in a new way. "They" are not doing this to "us". Our Free Will has not – and will not – be violated. We, the Ancient Ones, have been incarnating on Earth in greater numbers than any time before. We sit on the Galactic Council even as we sit on our dining chairs at home. We, as humanity, are being shown and guided on the path to being kinder, more spiritually aware, and more connected at the heart level with all of creation by our own higher selves.

With the assistance of our own selves as Lightworkers, including reiki practitioners, and energy healers, we – as our higher selves – are healing humanity, clearing our karma, unleashing humankind from an unhealthy over-connection to lower chakras, and moving the collective consciousness ever higher. This takes place with the assistance of everyone who is being kind and caring, compassionate and loving. In so many ways, we all are Lightworkers the moment we turn away from separation and fear.

As intuitive Reiki Masters, Lightworkers, and Nova Gaia Love Energy Healers, we three Cartographers of the New World are blessed to have a front row seat on the changes that are taking place as the past, present, and future become one. While giving healing sessions and in meditation, we uncover trends and messages that are not just true for the recipient, but are truths for us to share with other Lightworkers and humanity as a whole.

As you read, you will gain a clearer understanding of the cycle of energetic growth and change that continually occurs as people release their old ways and leap courageously into the unknown to explore and create something wonderful and new. You will grow on the path of Nova Gaia in your own perfect way. Somewhere in these pages you will recognize yourself and the messages meant for you. When that happens, suddenly things in your life and the lives of those around you take on a whole new meaning.

In this map, we share real life experiences from meditations, channelings, and healing sessions we have given, and the messages contained therein. Then we guide you through energetic download experiences for your own personally unique healing and lessons.

As prophetic visions, most of the experiences we relate were received during traditional reiki sessions while we, the Cartographers, existed in the 4D void, bridging the gap from 3D to 5D, with glimpses beyond. These messages guided each of us Cartographers of the New World so we could recognize the emerging Nova Gaia energies and understand the changes we were observing in ourselves and others.

We are grateful for the role reiki has played in our lives, preparing and leading us to this point to propel us into Nova Gaia Love Energy and Nova Gaia Love Energy Healing.

Energy change happens at different times for different people. There is no sense of being more evolved or less evolved, only a sense of perfection unfolding in its perfect way. Some of the messages and experiences in the pages ahead will be part of your past. Others will exist in your present or be part of your future. You are at the exact perfect place in your development to fulfill the role Spirit and your Higher Self (or, more accurately, Spirit AS your Higher Self) has set before you.

We are the Masters of how this
Map is written.
You are the Master of how this Map
serves you.

No two paths through this Map
are the same.

How to Use This Map

We are the Masters of how this Map is written.
You are the Master of how this Map serves you.

This is a concept you will see repeated many times throughout our many Maps of Nova Gaia, for the true essence of the Nova Gaia energy proves again and again that your path is your own. You are not here to follow others, to mimic their talents and skills. You are here to absorb what is right for you when it is right for you. Take what you need and leave the rest for another time.

That being said, you will find yourself delving into this Map time and time again, for each chapter is not just a chapter. Each chapter is a lesson that ends with a personalized energy download experience. We do not direct this experience. We are simply the portals bringing this opportunity for your spirit to engage with the Nova Gaia energies of the highest level that you are able to receive at this moment.

In the initial chapters written by The Angel, simply read the passages, relax, and allow the energy to fill you. The Fairie's middle chapters are followed by powerful mandalas for you to gaze upon. These act without words to fill you with the essence of the Divine. The last chapters from The Dragon Heart are active meditations that allow you to travel through all time and space even as you read them.

It is recommended that you write down notes of your download experiences, creating a personalized Map of your own to mark your progress on your traveled path. You may use a journal or in the print version of this Map you may write in the space provided. Write new notes each time you journey through this Map. It will amaze you to see the upward spiral of knowledge, awareness, and insight that comes to you.

You may find yourself jumping from one chapter to another in an order that is unique to you. That is Spirit guiding you. You may find yourself reaching for this Map out of the blue, opening it at random, and finding a precise insight that has been hidden and waiting for you to evolve into readiness to recognize its wisdom. This is Spirit guiding you. Many others will read this Map from beginning to end in the order that it is written. This is Spirit guiding you, just as Spirit guided us to create it in this order.

No two paths through this Map are the same. This is true even for you. Read it once and you will find yourself on one path. Read it again later and you will find yourself in new territory. Created through Divine Love, this Map is a miraculous tool for your own personal growth.

Act I ~ The Angel

During a few months in the Spring of 2018, I was granted access to incredible visions and lessons. These were given to me at that time specifically for you and your current Now experience of learning to live and interact with the Nova Gaia energies. These visions came primarily while I worked as a volunteer Reiki Master at the local Cancer Center, sharing healing energy with a number of patients and staff. I also received some of these special messages while meditating or giving healing sessions to family and friends.

At the Cancer Center all reiki volunteers follow a protocol of set hand positions to be given in a prescribed order. You will hear these hand positions referenced again and again in the pages before you. As a rule, I far prefer to use my intuition to guide my hand placements during healing sessions. In all healing work, your Spiritual guidance is your truest teacher, your most compassionate partner, and your most faithful friend.

What I saw during these sessions is true for you now. It was an incredible honor to be entrusted with these experiences and to keep them in safekeeping for this very moment. May they bring you the growth you are seeking.

And now your journey continues with...

Experiences of The Angel in her human form.

Now your journey continues

Softly, Sweetly

As I settle into my chair at the head of the reiki table in the reiki room at the local Cancer Center where I volunteer, a gentle rain falls outside, unusual here in the arid desert. I enjoy the sound of the raindrops as I use the distance symbol, initiating energetic contact with the middle-aged woman lying before me.

Placing my hands gently over her closed eyes, I invoke Usui Reiki's mental/emotional symbol through both mental image and slight hand movements. Immediately, I hear the words, "softly, sweetly" in my mind.

These two simple words repeat over and over again as I move through my first few healing hand placements. "Softly, sweetly." "Softly, sweetly."

Neither male nor female, the voice saying the words is low and gentle, guiding and filled with Love.

On its own, my head starts to tilt, first to one side, then a few minutes later, over to the other. This is tempering the amount of energy flowing from Divine Source through my Crown Chakra.

Softly and sweetly, this delicate energy is careful not to overwhelm the woman before me as it infuses her with a soft, unfocused healing power.

Softly, sweetly.

Over the past few weeks, I have been guided to use the mental/emotional Symbol almost exclusively during all of my healing sessions, whether on myself, a person, or an animal. This is holding true now.

Mental and emotional healing seems to be what is needed most right now, and I am listening. I want to add additional symbols, but I know that is my own personal want, not Divine guidance, so I continue to let the mental/emotional healing flow uninterrupted and pure.

I am trusting my intuition fully and completely.

Moving from my lady's head to her throat chakra, still floating in the energetic peace of the mental/emotional symbol, I see a beautiful butterfly... at least that's what it appears to be at first.

Something isn't quite right. I focus up close on the image I see in my mind's eye and discover that it is not a butterfly at all. The insect I see in my mind's eye is much smaller than a butterfly.

I lean in closer with my consciousness. There are glassy wings and a buzzing sound. I pull my inner vision back a bit and see the long proboscis of a mosquito.

Before the session, this lovely lady told me she was not having pain directly, but she has been experiencing a lot of discomfort from peeling skin following her radiation treatments. Spirit reminds me that this is significant.

Ah! This mosquito could represent that irritating discomfort. The annoyance, the troubled skin. I feel more deeply into this thought to see if there is truth to this and if so, do I need to remove the mosquito?

No detailed answer appears regarding the particular effect of the mosquito, but I am led to understand that the mosquito represents an annoyance my lady does not need.

I am to remove the mosquito.

Calling in an advanced reiki symbol, I prepare my client's energy body for mosquito removal. Next, my hands form the second advanced symbol.

The action of this second symbol performs the actual removal. Surprise! As I watch, the symbol morphs into a fly swatter! But instead of swatting the mosquito, it acts like a spatula and flips this pesky annoying energy out of her energy field to a place where it can be cleansed, cleared, and repurposed for a higher use.

Pest removal mission accomplished, I am ready to move to my next hand position when suddenly an angry little boy appears and punches me right in the face!

What is that all about?!

The punch doesn't hurt, neither physically, nor energetically. There is no actual fist hitting me, it is just a mental image, but what do I do now? Do I energetically smack the kid or use the energy of my advanced reiki symbols to release and remove him?

Again, I lean into my guidance for clarity and learn that the boy is not a problem to be removed. He is a survival strategy triggered by releasing the mosquito from my client's energy field.

The mosquito was an annoyance, but it was a familiar annoyance to my lovely lady. The mosquito was *her* annoyance to have and to hold dear.

Just as it was time to release that buzzing, biting cause of annoyance, it is time for this sullen little boy to be healed of his anger so he can be free to focus on more positive and productive activities. I focus on the boy and get ready.

Drawing a third advanced reiki symbol, the symbol of Divine Love, I channel the energy directly to the little boy, grateful that he is willing and able to receive it.

A few moments later, I get a visual image of this little boy happily swimming in a lagoon with turtles. I hear him laughing and splashing about. It is wonderful.

At my lady's abdomen I discover an angry bear on her left side. He's just come out of hibernation and is not happy one bit about being disturbed. I tell the bear he needs to eat something and take a nap.

I explain that when he wakes up he'll feel better. I give him a handful of berries and some kind of meat or pemmican to eat and send him back to his cave to go to bed.

On the right side of my lady's abdomen, my mind's eye sees a beautifully fertile field filled with sunlight and flowers. I feel a deep *knowing* that when the bear wakes up from his nap, he will be happy to frolic in this wonderful field.

I also know that this fertile field will be filling up both sides of my lady's abdomen when the bear wakes up again. As with the healing of the now-happy boy, this healing of the cranky bear represents the timely balancing and healing of my lady's masculine and feminine energies.

As I travel down to my lady's knees, I get a hint that something I've been seeing in my intuitive reiki sessions over the past few weeks is still holding true – She has no roots.

Typically, I see roots growing out from the bottoms of my clients' feet, long, strong, and deep. These extensive roots go far down into the Earth and represent stability and a belongingness to both time and place.

In the last few weeks, however, I've only seen broken and dying roots, until ultimately there have been no roots at all. Absolutely none.

In the past, thin, broken, or malformed roots were a sure sign that healing was called for and I would focus the healing energy specifically for that purpose, but in these past weeks I've been told to let them be.

This session is no different.

It is made abundantly clear to me through *knowing* that I am not supposed to work on growing, establishing, or connecting new roots for my lady or anyone else in any way at this time.

Getting this information while I am at my lady's knees is a heads up, so I won't go into root-healing mode when I get to her feet. But first her knees have their own story to tell.

Your knees tell you where to go. My lovely lady's knees show me a visual of a bored kid sitting in an old-fashioned phone booth, waiting and waiting for an important call. The call that will give him directions on when and where to go.

The call that hasn't come through even after an extremely long year of waiting.

This kid is no fool. He is fed up with hearing the promise that the call will come "soon". He is demanding that this empty promise put up or shut up!

Only... it's not an empty promise. And he really is closer to getting the call than ever before.

He doesn't know it, but he's waiting to learn his new role for the New Earth. It's just too soon. His new role is too unformed for the call to go out or for those directions to be firmed up.

The wait goes on.

I've come across other knees in the past few weeks that were cool, calm, and collected when it came to waiting. They are taking this hiatus in stride and going on vacation until it's time for action.

But not these knees. These knees are sick and tired of being bored. They want action! And they want it NOW!

There's not much action when you're at a roadside phone booth in the middle of nowhere.

Just like the angry little boy earlier, the phone booth boy needs a positive and productive activity to keep him occupied. His job for now is to wait and be ready to spring into action when the call finally comes.

I give the boy a little hand held game to entertain him, but even the best games get old after a while, so what then?

Fortunately, Spirit has an answer: Connection.

"Reach out your energy and connect with all of the other people waiting at their own phone booths," I was guided to say to the boy in the phone booth, encouraging him, "Communicate and play with them. There's a big grid-full of people in your same situation. You are not alone. And you don't need to clog the phone line to connect with them, just reach out with your senses."

I feel a little apprehension at sharing this advice, like I may be releasing something bigger and more powerful than I am comfortable with. Ultimately, I just have to trust Source and deliver the message to the phone booth kid, even if it gives me a queasy dose of the heebie jeebies.

At my lady's feet, as I'd been told to expect, there are no roots whatsoever. None. Words sound in my head to caution me, "Don't even try".

Then I am given specific instructions and a new sense of clarity on how to handle this rootlessness and prepare for the time when we finally do put down new roots.

The first part of the message is this: Ground UP. Instead of sending our roots deep down into the ground to stabilize us and provide us with a sense of security and place, this is a time for humanity to ground UP into the Heavens, our true home.

Secondly, it is stressed that each of us should focus on what we *want*. This focus should come not so much with our thoughts, but with our *feelings*, our emotions. Answer the question "What do you want to *feel* in your new energetic home?" with your heart and energy vibration.

The last part of the message is a recommendation that we take time to stand on the ground at the base of a tree and absorb the energy and information from the tree roots and soil's micro fungal grid up through our feet. Trees are far more advanced than human beings are in establishing and adapting to the New Earth.

By standing at a tree's roots and sensing their energy, we can each get a feel for newer Earth energies directly, guiding us to find our individual way to a higher level - A higher level we identify with our energetic senses and choose independently with no other human interference, no sense of obligation or expectation.

Softly, Sweetly Download Experience

There are so many lessons to be gleaned from this teaching. Now is the time for you to receive the lessons and energy it holds specifically for you. Sit or lie back comfortably and allow the energies to fill you now. Let your mind wander over the story you have just read, following any topics or pathways that open to you, no matter how strange. You may fall into a deep sleep and be completely unaware of the lessons and energies that come to be integrated. Do not be concerned. You will receive exactly what is right for you at this time.

Notes

Notes

Discovering a Diamond

Placing my hands gently at the head of the gentleman lying on the reiki table in front of me, I immediately see a stormy ocean crashing against jagged rocks. An agitated sea lion barks at the waves, barely audible over the crashing uproar of the storm.

Using the Usui Reiki mental/emotional symbol combined with the power symbol, I calm the waves and watch as the sea lion jumps into the water.

Now it is night on the ocean. Calm and still, with very dark, deep water. It doesn't feel ominous. It just feels like waiting...

I can see the full moon shining, but there is something else, some other form of light. I focus deeper to find out what this form of light is.

It is a searchlight panning across the expanse of the vast ocean, searching, searching for something, but what?

I look around for the sea lion and find him sleeping on a sandy beach, completely oblivious to the searchlight on the dark water.

I am prompted to use my higher level energy symbols for the removal of old karma, but I am not sure what I am removing. The darkness? The searching? I will never know. I activate the symbols for removal.

What I do learn is that my gentleman needs to fill his mind with new thoughts. He needs to be interested and engaged in a new pursuit. This pursuit needs to go beyond the thought level.

Specifically, he needs to use his hands in a creative activity in order to balance his ranging thoughts and emotions. This knowledge fills me as I move through various hand positions, the energy flowing smoothly and easily.

Suddenly I am prompted to use the advanced symbol for Knowing Yourself and a sudden new knowledge instantly fills me along with a familiar energy.

My gentleman is a Diamond! I can see his Diamond Energy, bright and shining, small and lodged down low in his solar plexus.

Being a Diamond is a serious business. I am one. You may be one, too. There are many different variations, colors, and depths in Diamond Energy.

Diamond Energy is a certain specialized energy some people carry. It shines out to heal and grow a more beautiful world filled with kinder, more aware people.

As Diamonds, we don't have to DO much, we just have to tend this energy and BE, allowing this energy to grow and shine forth. Somewhere along the line, we connect into the world grid of Diamonds to support each other and envelop the Earth with this special Diamond Energy.

Not everyone is a Diamond. There are other kinds of amazing energies out there as well and every single one of them is needed.

Recently, I did a reiki session on a person with bright Sunflower Energy that follows the sun and fills people with joy and optimism. I also did a session on a woman with gentle Pearl Energy. She was filled with pearls of wisdom and her energy helps others in her vicinity have epiphanies and recognize their own personalized words of wisdom.

In all cases, as this special energy matures, it reaches out and has an impact in an ever expanding radius, reaching out for miles. But for each of us it starts out small. And for my gentleman, it begins with this session.

As I place my hands at my gentleman's abdomen, I am overwhelmed by the rush of energy flowing through me to activate his Diamond Energy. This is not reiki energy, but something much higher and stronger. This strong energy makes me nauseated and my legs feel weak, but it only lasts a brief moment before this incredible new energy moderates itself and flows deeply.

I can see his little Solar Plexus Diamond start to sparkle and shine with a clear white energy that has flecks of blue and prismatic rainbow specks.

Beautiful!

At his knees, I learn that my gentleman has not been fully connected to his earthly body.

Interesting, I wonder why?

Even before this question is finished forming in my mind, I see my answer in a previous life view.

I see a nursemaid, possibly Flemish, back in the 1500's or 1600's. She is holding a tiny newborn babe. The expression on her face as she looks down at the bundle in her arms and clucks her tongue makes it clear that the baby in her arms isn't likely to live.

My gentleman was that baby.

Then I see a face without a nose.

The noseless face isn't scary. In fact, it's almost comical, but I know there's a message here for me to figure out. How does this relate? The little baby I saw had a nose. The baby wasn't disfigured at all. It just weakened and died.

Suddenly, I get it: The baby didn't like being in human form and losing his full Spiritual senses. It was like being born without a nose, without a sense we take for granted as part of a full life. He preferred his friends and experiences in the Spirit World, so he didn't stay.

That experience was still haunting him, but it was now time for the karma of that past to be brought to the surface and healed so he could more fully inhabit this body and enjoy his new Diamond Energies without letting past experience draw him inexorably towards a return to Spirit once again.

I use the first four advanced energy symbols once again to remove the feelings and mistrust issues related to that earlier birth and Spirit World attachment experience.

His ankles assure me that he will be able to fully assimilate his new Diamond energy and become more engaged and interested in his current life. I see him looking like a teenager, visiting at a friend's family dinner table, full of excitement and plans, fully engaged in being a vibrant part of life.

At his feet, I can feel the difference in his energy. True to the common thread of the experiences of recent weeks he has no roots, but that's okay.

For a moment I am concerned when I feel my gentleman being enclosed in a cave. I invoke a newer, more advanced energy and see a hole appear in the top of the cave.

A strong violet light comes through this hole, direct from the higher levels of Heaven. This light is filled with Divine Love. I can feel this energy being drawn UP through him to ground him into the Heavens, replacing any and all need for roots for now.

It is glorious!

Closing the session, I feel a need to send energy to his "egg", my playful term for the auric energy field that surrounds each and every one of us.

As I send healing energy to his egg, I can very clearly feel his new Diamond Energy at work, establishing itself and bringing new healing to him at deeper levels. This Diamond Energy is invoking a healthy flow of energy in the shape of a Taurus – this energy flows in through his crown, down through his body, out through his feet, and on up in a circle around him to go down through his crown again and again in perpetual motion.

I can feel his Spirit Guides circling around me, admiring this clean new flow of energy. As the session ends, his Spirit Guides break into rousing cheers of delight and congratulations on our gentleman's tremendous progress and his successful new form of energy exchange.

Discovering a Diamond Download Experience

I know now that the higher stronger energy I felt while activating this gentleman was an early aspect of Nova Gaia Love Energy. Just as this man was activated as a Diamond, it is time now for you to be activated into your own unique signature energy. If you are already aware of your signature energy, this download experience will deepen your connection with the energy and broaden your understanding of the role your energy plays in the space around you. Sit or lie back comfortably, close your eyes, and invite the expansion of your innate energy to fill you. All signature energies have tremendous value. Be open and willing. This is why you are here.

Notes

In Harm's Way

Using the Usui Reiki distance symbol to connect energetically with the recipient, I begin this situation-based distance reiki session. I do not ask for any explanation of the situation. After all, it is none of my business. I am here to bring healing. Period. Finding out more would reinforce the old wound with gossip - that's how it feels to me, anyway. I trust that the reiki energy will tell me whatever I need to know, so I settle in and feel the energy flow.

Immediately I can sense that this healing relates to a situation from the past that has created years of grief, anger, and guilt for three different people.

I feel the connection primarily with the woman who has come to me for healing on this ghost from the past. Shortly thereafter, the other two players appear.

A secondary layer of people affected by this situation come up. Rippling out into the expanding darkness, more and more layers of people involved or affected in some way appear, including office workers who processed paperwork relating to the situation and IT people who worked to keep the internet and various apps and programs running.

They are all here, no matter how minutely involved, ready to accept healing.

The three main players arrange themselves in a triangle, each facing outward at a different point of the triangle, completely unable and unwilling to face each other.

For years it has been easier to ignore the issue and let it fester deep in the background rather than face it.

It's not such a big issue, really. The triangle is only about four feet long on each side and the problem, itself, fits neatly inside. The problem is kind of grey and amorphous, floating there with a sickly tint of yellow, being ignored.

Ignored, *ha*! Each primary player is fully aware of it. Every once in while this situation rears up and runs around the inside of the triangle, keeping each player awake, ruminating and angry.

Until now. It is time to deal with this mess and knock it down to size. I activate the first advanced healing symbol to initiate the healing, creating a safe space and expanding the energy bodies of all involved. This allows the dark emotion of festering mental memory to be removed and the wound healed. But before I can activate the next symbol to remove the damage and its cause, the three players have some business to attend to.

Healing doesn't happen with the wave of a magic wand or an energy-filled palm. Healing is not a Get Out of Jail Free Card. You have to do your own work. It cannot be done for you without your participation. With this safe expanded space created, the three main players reluctantly turn to face the center of the triangle and look at the issue. Together.

Their defenses immediately come up as each one goes into victim mode. They yell at each other. No matter which words these people use, energetically it all sounds the same.

"I'm the one who was wronged! You deceived me, you hurt me. You stabbed me in the back!" Fingers point from everywhere, "You, You, YOU! *You* are to blame! *I* am the innocent one here!"

I use the mental/emotional symbol along with a master symbol boost to calm the situation, then I quickly draw an additional symbol for Divine energy. The connecting lines of the triangle spring to life.

For the very first time, these three people are not looking at the situation from their own individual perspectives. With the aid of Divine energy's beautiful golden connecting lines of the triangle, they can finally see the situation from EACH OTHER'S perspective.

These three people are finally *seeing* the whole issue. And it isn't pretty. Not at all.

Selfish, dictatorial, lying, shamed, heartless, deceitful, manipulative, foolish, stupid. They feel the sting of each of these perceptions. Recoiling as if from a slap, the three figures look hollow-eyed and chastised. As if speaking with one voice, they extend their hands towards each other and say, "I am a terrible person. I did that mean, hurtful thing. I caused you real harm."

The three figures slump under the onslaught of their shadow selves, seeing themselves, not as victims, but as awful, horrible people. It is a crushing experience.

I draw the advanced symbol for Knowing Yourself and repeat its mantra three times. It is true that these three people had done some horrible things, but they weren't horrible people. In the grand scale of things, the entire situation was really pretty minor.

It is time for them to *know* themselves as they truly, truly are. It is time to put this issue into perspective.

Divine energy charges in as a bright, blindingly white light, amplifying the knowledge that is already there, existing inside each of the three people involved.

"But... I am a good person."

This feeling grows and grows in the pure white light, coming into perfect balance with the "I'm a terrible person. I did that mean, hurtful thing. I caused real harm" thoughts.

Positive and negative thoughts blend into a new understanding, an integration of the Shadow Self, a recognition that we are ALL Good People at heart.

"Yes! Yes!" my heart sings as the figures at the triangle stand taller and prouder, "That's it!"

As the healing energy diminishes and the light dims, the triangle is smaller and the three players stand close to each other with tears in their eyes.

But there is something else I can sense, something elusive. I lean in for better understanding.

Ah! That is it!

Each person is holding back a secret, a shame connected to this shared event.

Quick work with the advanced symbols of Divine Love and Peace makes it safe for each of the three to bring these hidden aspects forward, to own them, and to openly confess them. These secret shames are the aspects that had the power to keep these three people awake nights, even after all these many years.

Invoking the advanced energy symbol for Removal to clear up any last remnants of emotion connected to the events of the past seems like the right thing to do, but it is not needed. The trio now shares the lead for this session as I watch and provide support.

The three key players have completed the necessary healing work themselves. They come together, hugging, crying and laughing at the same time.

"I am so sorry I hurt you, I had no idea how you felt."

"I didn't understand what my actions did to you, how they harmed you for so many years."

"I've been so ashamed of being so stupid, I could only be angry at you. It was my way to try to protect myself from admitting how insensitive I was."

Each asks the others for forgiveness, forgiveness their hearts have already given.

They turn to face outward once again, but the three now stand together. They have each other's back.

Holding their hands palms up, they radiate healing energy to all of the secondary, tertiary, and other extraneous people who have been affected in some way by the past actions, thoughts, and emotions related to the old situation.

A few minutes later, the energy flow diminishes and I silently close the session.

Later, the woman who scheduled this situation-based distance reiki session reported that she is now sleeping very soundly and peacefully. She is able to think of the situation and move on to other thoughts and topics without going into a downward spiral of negative thoughts and feelings.

This woman has now accepted the situation as a part of her life in balance with all other parts of her life. It no longer has power over her.

In Harm's Way Download Experience

You have deep healing to accomplish, broader perspectives to see. This is an important and unavoidable part of your advancement. Cast about in your mind for a situation, large or small, which continues to cause you hurt or resentment. Sit or lie back comfortably, close your eyes, place your hands on your heart and focus on feelings of Love, peace, and acceptance. Now, in your mind, bring forth the main players in this drama of your past. Allow each player, including yourself, to speak of the pain that lingers from this situation of the past. Allow this to unfold. See your part of the pain as both a victim and as a perpetrator. You are safe to face the shadows of your life, as are the other people in your drama. Then heal together. Do not shy away from this important work. Know that you are protected, loved, and guided throughout this entire process.

Notes

Male and Female Balance

As this reiki session begins, I am immediately encouraged to use the symbol of Divine energy. Drawing the symbol and repeating its mantra three times reveals the vision of a violet flame coursing through the body of the gentleman lying on the reiki table in front of me.

Only I do not see his body as his body.

In my mind's eye, I see violet flames ripping through a large field of wild grasses. As the flame burns, it devours all weeds, leaving the different grasses and flowers intact.

Changing hand positions, I notice movement in a rocky area of the field and go in my mind's eye to investigate.

In amongst the rocks a coyote is eating a rabbit. My presence does not disturb his feast.

Strangely, I do not feel called upon to take action. I simply watch and trust the Divine energies that flow strongly and effortlessly from my hands.

But what is this I am witnessing? What is the meaning, the lesson, of this vision?

As I search, it becomes clearer.

The rabbit had been a scared rabbit in life. He represented my gentleman's fear.

The coyote, a scavenger, an opportunist, was feeding off of that fear, manipulating my gentleman and feeding off of his fear to keep him from fully living and embracing life.

Shortly after recognizing this truth, I notice another movement from the corner of my eye.

I cannot tell what it is at first, but as this movement comes closer the coyote takes one look, flinches, and quickly runs off.

It is a man, a large man, with his back to the sun.

It's not a prehistoric man, not a Native American as we know them, but something – SomeONE – in-between. Some kind of large, well-muscled aboriginal man.

One of the Ancient Ones, this man is born of desert and mountain and stream.

As he stands there, I am guided to invoke the advanced reiki symbol for Knowing Yourself.

Know Yourself, Know Yourself, Know Yourself. I repeat the symbol's mantra three times.

Ah! This Ancient One is bringing a gift. He is bringing back the original pattern, the original blueprint of strength and mastery for my gentleman.

Placing my hands near my gentleman's throat area, I see a volcano, but it isn't like any volcano I have ever seen before.

Angry red lava does not flow out at all.

Soft blue and white water flows UP from the surrounding land, UP to the mouth of the volcano. This water cascades beautifully into the mouth of the volcano forming a circular waterfall to the center of the crater.

It is the light blue water of absolute truth. It is the sweet white water of purification.

This water flows inward to extinguish a constant, unpredictable volcanic anger. This cascading water flows in to bring peace and understanding.

Moving to the torso, I notice a slight headache at the front of my skull. This headache is shaped like a "T". It is telling me to place my hands in a T form on my gentleman's chest to get energy simultaneously to his heart and thymus.

A roaring lion's head appears, agitated and concerned about any energy removal. He is adamant that I should not remove anything that "makes me, ME."

But am I *supposed* to participate in any energy removal?

Should I use advanced energies to remove the anger, the fear, or anything else? I've done it before plenty of times, but this is *this* time. Am I meant to play an active role or do I just observe, hold space, and allow the healing energy to flow through me from Spirit to my gentleman?

I ask Spirit for guidance. If I hear "Yes", I will negotiate with the Lion head to see what he is willing to release.

I clearly hear Spirit say "No".

My personal participation in this healing is not about the removal of anything. Divine energy is taking care of that end of things. I am here to be the conduit and to bring in the energy of Love, security, and trust.

Throughout this session, I bring in different symbols as guided. Usui symbols for transcending time and for mental and emotional healing, plus the power and Master symbols. Advanced symbols for Flow, for Peace, for Divine Love, for Knowing Yourself.

The energy flows smoothly and strongly.

Female energy flows comfortably into the right side of my gentleman's ribcage. This is energy for nurturing oneself, for emotional expression and healing. Male energy flows into his left side.

Traditionally, the right side represents male aspects and the left, female. In this case, however, it is the opposite as these energies are being balanced and blended for greater harmony. Female energy flows into the right and male energy flows into the left.

Various senses, images, and words shift and merge. A sense of peace, balance, and symbiosis grows. A recognition that increased female energy and standing in the world does not mean diminished male energy and standing.

The strong knowledge that a rising tide lifts all boats is present and undeniable.

The rising tide of female energy in the world is bringing balance to a way of life that has been severely off kilter. Removed from the warped perspective of duality, female energy and power is a benefit to be cherished by all. It is in no way a threat to men.

Understanding comes that men and women alike are being tricked and oppressed by falsely created, bloated, greedy, unnecessary, controlling systems and policies due to this ongoing lack of balance in male/female energies in the world.

It is changing rapidly right now, coming beautifully into balance. But adaptation to the new blend of energies has been hard for many, my gentleman included.

I send reassuring energy and comfort.

You are not being made less. You are being made whole.

Healing energy shows itself as a strong green light. At my gentleman's abdomen, his bile ducts call out for healing and balance so they can provide better regulation of bile.

Moving to the leg positions, I see my gentleman's knees knitting while rocking in rocking chairs. They look like old grannies on a porch, just passing time.

We are still in a period of waiting for the New Earth to be firm enough for us to make plans, firm enough to choose a direction and to go forward.

My first impression at reaching my gentleman's ankles is one of strength and stability. But on further inspection, I find that the inside of the bone is like gummy bears or Swedish fish. Jellied candy ankles, jiggly and non-supportive. They are stable for now, but too much of the future is insecure for them to truly be firm.

I let the healing energy flow and trust it to do what is needed at this time.

At my gentleman's feet, I draw a symbol for grounding, but like most of my reiki clients lately, he has no roots to ground him into the Earth. Instead, a beautiful blue light appears from the Heavens and my gentleman began to ground UP into the Heavens.

This blue light of Truth and Divine Love has a message for my gentleman that repeats over and over again: "You are Complete. You are Precious. You are Whole. You are Everything I Could Ever Desire You to Be. Know Yourself. Know Yourself. Know Yourself."

As the session nears its end, I am drawn to work in the energy field surrounding my gentleman.

I feel my Healing Guide, Hagar, take over my hands, moving them where they need to go. This is a gentle process that I allow willingly and I watch my hands flow from position to position. It cannot happen without my permission.

Hagar guides my hands to work primarily on balancing and connecting the heart and root chakras. When the energy flow diminishes, it is time for me to finish and seal this healing session with Divine Love and wisdom.

With most in-person reiki sessions, I finish the session by moving my hands in a sweeping motion three times from the person's head to their feet, moving extraneous energy and debris down the body and out of the client's energy field. This time, however, that isn't needed. There is not a speck of debris to remove.

True to what Spirit told me near the beginning of the session, this isn't a session for removal. It is a session for peace, security, and understanding.

Moving my hands towards my gentleman's Crown Chakra to begin the sealing process, I get a quick image of a can of sardines being opened, the key turning to curl open the metal top and reveal the contents.

"No! Not yet!" a voice cries and the sardine can seals itself back up in an instant. We are getting closer to being able to see into our future on the New Earth.

This particular gentleman loves his healing sessions, but does not ask me to share any intuitive messages. I know that the energy will communicate all of the messages the client needs to hear or understand without my intervention.

This knowledge was reinforced the day after this session when I overheard this gentleman muttering to himself, "I don't know why I've always let so many things get to me, things that really don't matter."

Male and Female Balance Download Experience

The balance of male and female energies is an important precursor to the full experience of Nova Gaia. It is the forerunner of balanced integration of female and male. Sit or lie back comfortably and close your eyes. Breathe deeply and allow your mind to wander as energy fills you and works to bring you into beautiful balance. There is no threat. There is no loss. There is only a more complete and perfect you.

Notes

Notes

Pax et Bonum

This session was... odd. Not my usual intuitive style at all. It happened on April 1st, an important energy day - and month - of integrating and assimilating the huge energy upgrades from the preceding weeks.

I initiate connection through reiki's distance symbol with the client lying in front of me on the reiki table and POW! Image after image starts to flash before my mind's eye, rapidly going from one to the next with no apparent rhyme nor reason.

Could they be memories of this and other lives? Old junk coming up to be kissed goodbye as we step into the New? Or new, updated versions of past memories that have been modified to better suit this New Earth we now inhabit?

I wish I had the answer to that, but I don't. I'm as flummoxed now as I was then.

I take a deep breath, center myself, and do exactly what I am supposed to do – I allow both the images and the reiki energy flow. For this session, I am only a peripheral participant and observer, much more removed from the process than I usually am.

It is strange.

In healing work it is always important to set your personality and ego aside and let the energy give its blessing without the practitioner getting in the way, but as an Intuitive, I am typically brought into the session in additional ways so I can better do my job as an energy translator and messenger.

I prefer being involved in my sessions. It makes it more interesting for me, but I have also had many experiences where I simply enjoy the feeling and flow of the energy without receiving images, colors, words, scents, and whatever else Spirit sends my way. This particular session, however, was a strange blending of both.

All through the hand positions on my client's head, images flash quickly from one to another with no apparent link or trend, but once I place my hands at his heart, this changes.

It is amazing!

I see beautiful blue-white light forming a cross with singing Angels gathering around it.

Grace.

A feeling of peace and holiness washes over me and I bow my head in humility and gratitude.

Three words. I hear three words. An unseen voice says the three glorious words. "Pax et Bonum."

The Franciscan Order's version of "Aloha," Pax et Bonum is a blessing used in both greeting and farewell. It means "Peace and All Good to You." Pax et Bonum... Pax et Bonum... Pax et Bonum...

Throughout all of the healing hand placements at arms and torso, I invoke higher level symbols for Peace and for Divine Love, saying their mantras at times, the words Pax et Bonum at others.

In each instance, I repeat the words three times to bring the energy down from the highest reaches throughout all of the energy levels, down to the physical body. But this is not Reiki energy that is flowing.

I am participating in a blessing from Above.

Reverently, I place the peaceful healing energy deep into the human form lying before me on the reiki table.

This energy symbolically appears as solid golden light, a light that absorbs fully into the body on my reiki table. Over and over again, I hear "Pax et Bonum... Pax et Bonum...Pax et Bonum..."

At my gentleman's knees there is white light, a light so bright and blinding that nothing can be seen or discerned.

"Just be," the energy says, "Just be in this moment."

There is no forward, there is no back, there is no path to follow or direction to choose, there is simply this New Earth energy, changing everything in divinely subtle ways.

This light and feeling continues as I move through the remaining leg positions, but when I arrive at the bottoms of my gentleman's feet, I am in for a surprise. Roots!

He has roots! Long, deep roots! But these are roots like I have never ever seen before.

These aren't the same kind of long, deep roots I used to see in the Old Earth energy. This is something different.

I see multiple little roots, woven and braided together to be strong and deep. I follow the roots down and see something else that is new: Every time the roots come to a rock or obstacle, they separate, go around the obstacle on all sides, then join together beneath the obstacle and braid up again.

I let out a sigh. It feels so nice to see roots in the ground again. We are moving forward, even as we find ourselves "just be"-ing in this present moment.

Pax et Bonum.

Pax et Bonum Download Experience

This is a deep and peaceful blessing for you from the highest reaches of Heaven. Sit or lie back, close your eyes and relax. Wait patiently, repeating the words "Pax et Bonum" to yourself until you begin to feel the energy enter you from above. Allow and embrace this. Continue to repeat the words to yourself or be silent, whatever your natural guidance leads you to do. Just be in this moment.

Notes

Psychic Surgery

My gentleman of Peace and All Good returned a few days later for another session. The mass of energy hitting all "Sensitives" in the past week had left him feeling both tired and spacey.

This gentleman is very energy-sensitive, but is not especially open to hearing about energy and intuitive messages. Sometimes he wants to know what's going on in the "woo woo" world, but for the most part energy talk sounds crazy to him. Regardless of his mood, however, he still comes back for energy healing.

A person does not have to be open to the world beyond what can be touched and seen in order to receive the benefits of energy healing. This gentleman loves the feel of the healing energy. He loves the way the energy relaxes him and recognizes how it helps him with his health.

Once again, this was an unusual session.

Upon connecting with my gentleman and starting the flow of reiki energy, I am informed in no uncertain terms that this session is not about the removal of anything old, negative, or unwanted.

This session is all about receiving.

First and foremost, I am told just to observe and keep out of the way. Spirit has some important work to do.

I stand, holding safe, loving space at my gentleman's head. I am simply a conduit, letting the healing energy flow. While I send reiki, a new energy fills the healing space that surrounds and envelops the form on the table before me.

I observe as a long incision appears, running all along the center of his torso. Some form of surgery is about to take place. Before this operation starts, a poem begins to run through my head:

Holy Fire, Holy Love,
Holy Blessings From Above

This poem repeats itself in a kind of chant throughout the entire surgical procedure.

While I watch, the skin on my gentleman's torso is split down the middle and pulled back to each side. I witness his intestines being lifted up and out by unseen hands and gently placed at his left side. Now his liver rises up from his body and is set neatly at his right side.

His body is prepared and ready.

A Surgeon gowned in white appears and begins to work with needle and thread on something deep inside my gentleman. This surgeon spends quite a lot of time, working intently, carefully, plying his needle.

A being who is assisting with the surgery leans over to me and whispers in my ear that the surgeon is sewing up the black hole that has long existed inside my gentleman.

It is a black hole that sucks in all the Love my gentleman receives so no matter how much he is loved, no matter how much Love he receives, it never feels like enough. In fact, receiving Love rarely feels like being loved at all.

Now the surgeon holds his palm out, ready for the tool he needs for the next phase of this crucial operation.

A skilled psychic surgery nurse efficiently places something on the surgeon's outstretched hand. It appears to be a golden chafing dish.

The surgeon places this golden dish carefully inside my gentleman at the base of my gentleman's sacral chakra. With delicate stitches made of the strongest sinew, the surgeon sews this golden dish in place.

That done, my gentleman's liver and intestines are returned to their proper places and his skin is magically made whole again. The black hole is gone. The golden chafing dish will catch and hold Love whilst providing protection.

Protection from what? I wonder.

The assistant explains.

This black hole had been so vast a great deal of work was needed to close it. Even with the power of the most skilled psychic surgeon, this wound will take time to heal.

This wound needs to be protected so this black hole will not be called back. It is far too easy for my gentleman to willfully rip his stitches and bring back the feeling of being unloved that is his faulty "normal." The protection is not to protect against outside forces. It is to protect my gentleman from *himself.*

At this stage in psychic surgery I typically call in the higher reiki symbol of Divine Love to remove the void created and fill all space with Love so the client feels no sense of lack or loss. This time, however, I am specifically told to stay back and not interfere.

As I work through my remaining hand positions, I am repeatedly cautioned NOT to focus on filling my client up with Love.

This gentleman has lived without a sense of being loved for so long, it would be highly unnatural for him to be filled with Love all at once. My eyes fill with tears.

Like a man-made lake, his reservoir of Love needs to fill over time with a natural rainfall of Love. Anything else would be extremely uncomfortable, confusing, even painful to him.

My guides stress that my gentleman must first fill his reservoir with self-love. This is the only way he will be able to recognize true and actual heart-felt Love. It is the only path he can take that will lead him to being able to accept Love and to know that he is deserving of Love.

The session now focuses on healing the spiritual swelling and tenderness caused by the surgery. The session focuses on strengthening the sutures.

One may think psychic surgery can be done in a way that includes perfect and immediate healing. That can be done, but it isn't always for the best. It takes time and a gradual increase in a person's spiritual range of motion to be truly adopted and effective. If the change comes on suddenly, people may feel frightened at the unusual sensations and push against the changes.

Feeling that you are loved in a deep and meaningful way for the very first time can be extremely stressful. It is better to allow the energy to do the work slowly, letting change progress more naturally. This typically happens in myriad little ways that are nearly imperceptible until the person looks back at their journey and realizes that tremendous change has been accomplished.

For the remainder of the session, I hear the message "Don't expect much."

I had seen and felt something life changing happen to the man lying on the table before me, but he will not jump off of my reiki table as a completely different, completely healed person. It will take time for the energy changes to integrate.

I am cautioned that over the next few days people around him will bear the brunt of his crankiness and short temper. My gentleman will be feeling off center. He will express that confusion in different ways, translating something he doesn't understand into tangible feelings he can recognize. Additionally, as his personal energy changes it will create crankiness in the people around him, since they also have to adapt to the difference in his energy body.

Two days after this session, my gentleman remarked to his wife, "I have a problem. I've been working on it over the last few weeks. All my life, I've always felt like I have to be right. Like I always have to be right in everything all the time. Otherwise I think I'm just not good enough. And that's not true. I'm trying to change that about myself."

Psychic Surgery Download Experience

I am standing at your head sending energy, holding space and anchoring stability for you. You are safe to proceed. Allow yourself to sit or lie back with eyes closed, inviting in the psychic surgery that will move you forward at this time. Allow sensations and images to run through you. Do not be surprised if you fall into a form of sleep. You are unlikely to understand the depths and details of what is happening, although some will. Be gentle with yourself and the people around you over the next few days and weeks. Major changes are taking place within and around you.

Notes

Notes

All Timelines Are Now

My gentleman returned a few days later for his next session. He began by thanking me with the words, "The more frequent sessions these past few months have really helped me so much with my stress. I'm noticing a real difference."

I settle in at the head of the reiki table, close my eyes, and the session begins. Almost immediately, I see large yellow eyes glaring at me from the darkness. Large pointy fangs appear beneath the eyes. Sharp, dagger-like claws come in from the sides.

It all looks very threatening, but I do not feel any fear. As I observe, I allow the reiki energy to flow.

This black panther in the darkness guarding my gentleman's head isn't here to attack me. He is here to warn me to stay back. He is very serious about this. Referred pain shows up first in my tooth, then in my ear, as a preview of what I can expect if I cross the line.

I take a deep breath and mentally state "Only what is mine stays with me."

As I do this, I send assurance to the panther that I will keep my distance, sending energy without intruding. The pain diminishes immediately, evaporating completely over the next two minutes.

The healing energy flows strongly, but I do not get any additional images or messages as I work on my gentleman's head. True to my word, I hold back and do not seek any. However, I make it clear that I will accept any intuitive messages that offer themselves.

At the Throat Chakra, I see a cartoon igloo built on top of an iced-over lake. A cartoon Inuit emerges from the igloo and starts ice fishing. What does this image mean? I cast around for some explanation or understanding, but nothing comes forth. I ask my Guides for clarification.

My mental vision now follows the fishing line down, down, down and suddenly I understand. It has nothing to do with the image at the surface of the ice. It is about the depth beneath the surface. Deep. The healing taking place isn't just regular deep. It is deeeeeep.

I focus solely on sending the highest level reiki energy for the highest and greatest good of my client, but at my gentleman's torso Spirit guides me to use reiki's Distance symbol exclusively. This symbol transcends both time and space. This time, though, distance is measured differently. It does not go back in time to heal anything, nor does it go forward in time to smooth the way. It goes DEEP. Deeeeep. Deep into space.

I hear the phrase "All timelines are now".

Just as I was warned at my gentleman's head, I am to stay out of the healing work going on, but instead of warning me away with pointy teeth, I am now sent to relax at Panera or Starbucks. My body is still standing by the side of the reiki table with my hands sending energy to the client, but in my minds' eye, I am having tea and a pastry at a nice, relaxed hangout, biding my time and letting my thoughts wander. As I finish the torso and arms and move to the leg positions, my tea break ends.

At my gentleman's knees, the energy feels oddly cold and I see grey, dead bone. Ganesh, the Ascended Master with the elephant head, appears and tells me not to be concerned about the dead appearance of the knees. All is going well. This is not something that requires healing.

Since all timelines are now, Ganesh explains, there is no future to go to. The knees generally tell us where to go. The legs and feet are usually about moving forward and stability, but so much is different with this transition to the energetic New World, there is nowhere to go. Not yet. This creates a void where stability is concerned. It does not feel like instability, per se, it is simply a void.

Our old framework of stability does not apply anymore. There is the suggestion of a feeling that when our futures appear, they will not look the same. It is not just that they will be different futures; the way we see or experience them will be on a completely different framework.

It is something we cannot understand yet, we have to wait and experience it as it evolves.

Strong, uniquely refined energy – is it reiki or something new? – continues to send as Ganesh explains to me that there have been so many energy downloads and changes lately, the knees, ankles, and feet have been essentially taken offline so they are not overwhelmed with the sheer amount and newness of the energy.

This gives the body a chance to integrate the changes at all levels, otherwise, it would be extremely uncomfortable.

This is true, not just for the gentleman before me, but for a vast swath of humanity. All is going very well, Ganesh continues to assure me. All of the Ascended Masters are very pleased with our progress. The "our" in this message includes more than humankind, as everything on Earth is being bombarded with these energy changes.

The image of Ganesh fades away, but his words continue to come to me, bringing additional clarity.

"The timelines of the past no longer have much influence," he says, "and timelines of the future have yet to be created. The emotional choices and growth of this current period will be used to create the new timelines of the future for each individual."

At the bottoms of the feet, I see what appears to be a simply-dressed young Japanese woman in a dark blue kimono. She is kneeling and kissing my gentleman's feet with great humility and gratitude. The gratitude she expresses is combined of thanks for traveling the rough path of the past, thanks for the courage to travel through the current turbulence, and thanks for traveling the beautiful unseen and unknown road that is even now being created for the future.

As I finish treating the bottoms of my gentleman's feet, this young woman transforms into the Ascended Master Kwan Yin. Without words, with only energy, she says the future will be composed of Humility, Gratitude, Peace, Love, and the Greatest Good for All.

I work on the field around my client to close the session. I feel something alien, something otherworldly. Suddenly, I remember a flashing image from one of this client's last sessions. It is an extraterrestrial making a sudden appearance at my gentleman's sacral chakra with the message that my gentleman should not be surprised if he re-establishes contact.

My gentleman did have prior alien experiences when he lived in another area, though he was never sure if these experiences were real or imagined. He even joked that he had had an alien implant in his leg. It was hard and oblong shaped and suddenly disappeared one night after having been in his leg for many years.

In my gentleman's energy field I balance his Solar Plexus and Sacral Chakras to his Root and Earth Star Chakras. I realize that the Earth Star Chakra has not made an appearance in my reiki healing sessions for quite some time, but regarding this, I know to listen to the Panther. I stay back and do not press forward to question this appearance of the Earth Star Chakra.

All Timelines Are Now Download Experience

As Ganesh stated, "The timelines of the future have yet to be created. The emotional choices and growth of this current period will be used to create the new timelines of the future for each individual." Sit or lie back and take some time to go deeeeep. Consider your future, either consciously or subconsciously. Do this without words. Use only your emotions. What emotional option do you choose? Feel into this.

Notes

Notes

Adolescence

The sound of crickets from the "Summer Night" setting on the white noise machine distracts me, so it takes a minute or two for my thoughts to settle in and focus. The energy, thankfully, isn't distracted a bit. It flows strong and warm. In fact, my lady on the reiki table remarks on the warmth of my hands the moment I place them over her eyes.

Normally calm and complacent, my lady has been having troubles. Back pain and basically not feeling like herself over the past few weeks. She tells me her temper has had a very short fuse these days. So far, she has been able to keep it in check so anger has not bubbled over into words she would come to regret.

This lady is a long time meditator and energy sensitive. These feelings of anger, irritability, and sadness are something she thought she had moved beyond long ago.

With my personal energy finally settling down, I mentally ask that the back pain of my lady be taken care of. Immediately, I sense that this issue will be worked on when I reach the hand placements for the lower torso. What I *hear*, however, is something very different.

A petulant voice whines in my ear, "The back pain is all about the bowels. Geez, lady, eat a bran muffin sometime, would ya? Go eat a prune."

Over the years, I have received messages from Divine realms in many ways. I immediately recognize that this whiny voice is not the voice of Spirit.

I invoke a high level reiki symbol to strengthen my connection to the Divine and to block any "less than" energies... but... something is not quite right. I already have protection from lower energies. This protection is built into the energy work I do, so it's automatic. Outside low-vibration entities can't obtrude.

This voice is not from a buttinsky lower-energy entity. So I set out to determine where this voice is coming from.

Is it me and my ego being cranky because of the cricket sound? Is it truly information to help heal her back pain? No. This lady eats a very balanced diet. The back pain is due to something else. Then it hits me. The voice is *her own* energy. Her own cranky, adolescent energy.

The massive amounts of New World energy coming in over the past weeks are changing her energy body. These changes have knocked her out of kilter. The difficulty is that she cannot go back to her old ways of being "in kilter" because these old ways and old energies are gone for good.

My lady, a high functioning energy sensitive under the old energy system, has to grow into the new energies. Until this happens, she will feel like a gangly hormonal teen with growing pains and exhaustion and lanky arms and legs that seem to bump into everything. Her emotions will zoom all over the place.

Momentarily, I see an oyster on the seafloor and understand that the healing energy of this session is going deep. There is no pearl in this oyster. In fact, this oyster is crabby. His shell mouth is open and he is telling me to beat it and stop poking my nose where it doesn't belong.

I leave the cranky oyster alone. I hold space, provide comfort, and stay back on the sidelines while letting the energy flow. I am led to understand that this need to stay on the sidelines isn't just a privacy issue for my lady. It is also a protective issue for me.

I have been experiencing these same major upgrades and changes to the new energies, myself. On the prior day, my Third

Eye Chakra – the chakra of intuition – was particularly affected with forehead itching and a day-long sinus pressure headache.

There are three good reasons for me to be blocked from seeing what is going on during this healing:

1. Because it does not concern me.
2. Because it is going deeper than I can safely comprehend at this time.
3. Because my third eye connection to the energy needs to rest and assimilate my own big changes.

As I work along my lady's torso, I see white. A wall of white that I am not to penetrate. I am just to keep the healing energy flow open so it can do its thing. This goes beyond the energy of reiki that I am used to.

As I am standing there, a figure in a chef's hat comes out from behind the white wall to peer at me close up, as if to say, "Who is this trying to butt in?" The chef hat stays the same, but the face underneath transforms from a minion to a crazy chicken to the Swedish Chef from The Muppets.

I continue with the session, seeing only the white wall, letting my thoughts drift. I feel the energy flowing from my hands become more and more specific and refined. At one point my drifting thoughts find me knocking on a neighbor's door, asking for a cup of milk. The neighbor takes the cup from my hand and returns moments later with my cup full.

I look at the cup of milk and something isn't quite right. There are grey ashes floating in the milk. I peer closer and see old cigarette butts floating in there. The message is clear: Butt out!

I hadn't been aware that I was trying to butt in. I know this client loves to hear the intuitive messages I receive. Perhaps at some level I was trying to make sure to have something "good" to share. I wasn't being as flowing and accepting as I thought.

This is a good lesson for me not to try to force things or feel that I have to impress anyone, but to truly and completely set my ego aside, listen to my guidance, and follow it. I am not the show. I am the conduit for the energy.

At my lady's legs I see white plastic replacement joints in her knees and ankles. These parts are very anxious to show me their extreme flexibility, but I have concerns that they will not be durable enough for the long haul.

"It's okay," they reassure me, "We're temporary."

This makes sense. To me, the legs are all about moving forward and right now, as I am made to understand it, we have no *forward* to move to. All is in flux. There are no timelines to the future. We are in a kind of chaos that doesn't have the panicky feel of typical chaos.

We are in a chaotic void. A place of complete nothingness. It is oddly uncomfortable, but necessary for now.

It is important to remember that this is temporary. Work is going on behind the white wall.

The chefs are bringing together all of their best ingredients to create the perfect combination for your next phase of life. That is what will create the timeline possibilities for each person as they go forward.

Our past timelines still exist, but they appear grey and removed, like old dusty VCR tapes left on a shelf somewhere. They can still be viewed, but you have to borrow or dig out the old equipment and plug it in in order to use these old tapes. You need an adapter cord, too, so the old equipment can attach to your new TV for viewing.

The bottoms of my lady's feet show me an ambulance filled with people. The siren is turned on and the ambulance is driving down the street.

My lady isn't *in* the ambulance. Her view is from *in front* of the ambulance.

She is leading the way! Guiding everyone to the hospital safely and efficiently. This fits perfectly. This lady is a person who has worked very hard on her own healing over the past three decades. Her current energy level is much higher than average. In this New Earth energy, she is already an adolescent while most people are energetically infants, children, or still in gestation.

Adolescence Download Experience

Unseen work is ready to take place, preparing you for new timelines. Sit or lay back and close your eyes. Accept and allow, request and receive this aid. Divine chefs are bringing together all their best ingredients to create the perfect combination of elements for your next phase of life. Focus on holding the feeling in your heart that is key for what you want to experience in this next phase.

Notes

Notes

Primary Colors

I perform a quick mini-session for a friend, moving rather quickly from one position to the next. I do not expect this session to result in any messages. In fact, I am not focusing on receiving intuitive messages at all. As I move through the hand positions, my friend and I are chatting about the things we had seen on our hike earlier in the day. As I work, Spirit informs me that there are a few things I need to share.

At the head positions I see close-up images of a child's drawings. I cannot see the whole picture, just portions. A bit of a house drawn as a square with a triangle on it. Stick figure people with big round heads and stick fingers. A woman with a triangle body. The round yellow sun.

Everything is drawn in red, blue, and yellow crayon. Primary colors. It is all primary colors and basic shapes. Line, circle, square, triangle. That is very significant. These are the building blocks of Sacred Geometry.

When I change position to the arm and torso positions, I see a different kind of children's artwork. These are not crayon drawings. This is painting.

Painting. Big brush strokes with tempera paints on oversized sheets of paper like we used to use back in kindergarten. The colors are still just red, blue and yellow.

There is a solid red background with a yellow square towards the lower left. A blue circle is slightly to the upper right. As I continue the healing treatment, the circle and square shapes go from being flat to being 3D. The shapes poke up from the red field. After a time, both shapes drift off the paper and float up a bit, then down, as if finding their proper place, their proper depth.

The motion feels very similar to the way I move my hands when I am feeling my way into the exact right placement to send energy in a person's energy field without physical touch. My hands float up and down to find the right depth for sending the energy, to find the level where the energy is most needed.

I am drawn to send reiki to my friend's Root Chakra. I feel a tremendous draw of the energy there.

This surprises me. For the past few sessions, I have been subtly guided to avoid treating the Root Chakra directly. This neglect of the Root Chakra has occurred so naturally, I had not been aware of it until this moment.

I recognize that Spirit knows exactly what to do. It has been guiding me gently away from an area that needed to go through its own death and rebirth without some well-meaning reiki healer attempting to interfere with a necessary process for this unprecedented time on Earth.

At the ankles, I see a metal joint with a partial extension above and below the joint itself. This metal joint is extremely flexible. I see it going up, down, and whirling around much farther than a normal ankle.

I find myself feeling glad that I am only seeing this metal construction instead of viewing an actual human ankle and foot hyperextending. To see a human foot move in all these directions would have made me sick to my stomach.

Sick to my stomach? This is an odd observation. Why would I think that? Why would I go from my accepting "in-reiki" observational point of view to a judgmental "out-of-reiki" view? Why does that thought come to my mind? I cast though the energy for clarification on this.

Ah! Spirit is pointing out that the new and strange, while amazing, can be nauseating or repulsive at first because it doesn't fit our normal parameters, our normal limits. Spirit is pointing out that the possibilities of the New Earth appear "impossible" compared to what we are used to.

Is this a vision of actual physical possibilities or is it a vision of the energetic possibilities in the New World? Nausea is a common side effect of big energy upgrades. It is so common, Lightworkers call it the Ascension Flu. Other cold and flu-like symptoms can show up as the Ascension Flu, too. You feel sick-ish, but you know you aren't sick.

Physical or energetic? I do not know the answer to this. What I do know is that we are going to have to open ourselves up to far greater possibilities than we are used to.

Primary Colors Download Experience

It is time to release your attachment to what you know. It is time to go back to the beginning, back to the basic building blocks, and begin to rebuild your connection to the energies that surround you with new blocks that have capabilities you have never dreamed of before. Sit or lie back, close your eyes, and allow Divine energy to fill you and guide you.

Notes

Notes

Let It Flow, The Future Is Coming On

Today's lady is feeling significantly better than she felt the last time I saw her. She is sure this is the result of her last reiki treatment. She practically flys onto the reiki table, ready to take in healing energy. I lay my hands on her head and immediately I hear The Beatles singing Let It Be, but the words are a little different.

"Let it Flow, Let it Flow, Let it Flow, Let it Flow. Speaking words of Wisdom, Let it Flow." So that's what I do. I calmly let the calm energy flow.

When I get to my lady's neck and shoulders, the music changes to Elton John's Crocodile Rock.

I know there is a message there, but I do not know what it is. What kind of message is in Crocodile Rock? What can it be? I listen while a part of the song plays over and over again in my head, trusting that Spirit will make it clear.

"While all the other kids were rocking 'round the clock, she was hopping and bopping to the Crocodile Rock, yeah!"

Ah! My lady is on a different time signature, a different rhythm. Sing "Rock Around the Clock", then sing "Crocodile Rock" and you will understand what I mean. Both songs rock, but Crocodile Rock has a very different energy to it.

At my lady's hands I see a vision of red jasper as the lyrics in my head sing "Holding Hands and Skimming Stones, Had an old gold Chevy and a place of my own". Holding jasper seems to be important.

Traditionally red jasper is used for grounding, but I am not certain that is what is specifically needed for this particular time. It is possible the red jasper is for stamina to see us through these changes. It has been a long haul of spiritual growth and increasing Earth energy. People are getting weary.

Now I see a little tripod, the kind used for firing pottery in a kiln. Look on the bottom of a vase or pot and you'll often see three little marks left by the tiny points of the little tripod stilts that hold the item off the bottom of the kiln. I also see a shark tooth. Both of these visions point to transformation, growth, and change.

As I work on my lady's torso, letting the healing energy flow, her body appears to be made of clay. Water begins to course down her entire body from top to bottom. The water is keeping the clay of her body moist and malleable.

My lady is not yet ready to be fired in the kiln. She can still be molded and changed. This is important. Once the clay is fired, it becomes set.

My mind drifts along, flitting from thought to thought. My own memories, imagined conversations. These float in and out of my head. The sounds of Let it Flow and Crocodile Rock continue to play over and over again.

The work going on is for the client alone. I am being kept occupied by these thoughts so I will not be a pest, trying to see or feel something that is not for me. The lady on the table before me and Spirit are working together to form the clay of her future, with no outer interference.

At her feet I am surprised when suddenly an elk appears, quickly transforming from an elk into a beautiful, proud stag. A purple amulet and a blast of turquoise color run down the stag's heartline while supremely bright light shines behind the stag. It is an indescribably awesome sight.

I move in for a closer look at the stag. As I peer at his head, he begins chewing his cud very calmly, taking everything all in stride.

When you are amazing, it is not that big a deal to you. You're just being you.

At the bottoms of my lady's feet, I see little, plump baby roots, like the chubby, adorable legs of a human baby. The wandering, exploratory roots of the past weeks appear to be gone. I feel like hugging her roots.

Just as I finish her session, a new song starts to play in my mind. A song by Gorillaz. "I'm happy! Feeling glad. I got sunshine in a bag. I'm useless, but not for long. The future is coming on. It's coming on. The future is coming on."

Let It Flow, The Future Is Coming On Download Experience

It is time. Time for you to flow into a different rhythm. Time for you to begin the work of different future timelines. Hope shines. Sit or lie back, close your eyes, and drift into the world between worlds. Let the energy fill you. As you experience the shining of hope, follow that shine, follow that hope, follow that light and see where it takes you.

Notes

Notes

Sewerline

While on vacation during this special Spring of Divine messages, I received some strong impressions I have been told to share with you...

The first night of the impressions I feel a tremendous energy flowing underneath me. I delve into the sensations and see a rushing river of dark water. It does not feel scary or threatening, just powerful. As I focus on this torrent the visual becomes stronger.

It is like a flowing river made of stone. Obsidian? Onyx? Black Tourmaline? I cannot be sure. This river is flowing underground, under us all. Everyone. So powerfully.

I keep thinking it is like some kind of sewer, but this makes absolutely no sense to me. This river is too beautiful and strong to be a sewer. The next day, however, proves my instincts right.

When I wake up the next morning, I can still sense this rushing torrent, but the water is thick, brown and turbulent, carrying bulky solid waste along at a tremendous rate. I can even see appliances being rushed along in the flood. Dishwashers, refrigerators, and ovens show their square edges in the fast-flowing muck.

This sense continues all day long. It isn't so much a flowing underground now, but a flowing behind my spine and behind the spines of everyone I see around me. This isn't all my own debris, but the effluvia and waste of everyone who needs to be clean and clear before the energy Event Horizon that is coming in a few days. (An Event Horizon is the outer boundary of a significant energy event)

Here we all thought we had all done so well and worked so hard to clear ourselves all these years! Ha! There is so much more to clear out. The river is just as brown and polluted at the end of the day as it had been first thing in the morning. While I was fully aware of the clearing movement going on, it didn't seem to have too much impact on me and my day… or did it?

I did not feel sick and dizzy or nauseated or sleepy, but my companions and I were all more on edge and crankier that day than three vacationing people should be.

The following morning, I awake and check in on the flow. The river does not have big chunks in it now. It flows a little less rapidly and is a yellowy brown color. This major flush is doing exactly what it needs to do. It continues all day in this manner and my companions and I are all in better spirits. I check in regularly throughout the day and the river is still clearing more of this liquid waste.

As I go to bed at night, I receive a preview of the next day's energy. I see a drain in the middle of a large field with the last curl of water from this once-massive stream circling the drain and gurgling down. The water is not crystal clear. It is still a little murky, a little agitated, but far, far cleaner than it had been before.

Throughout the entire next day this vision holds true. Just a last little bit of water gurgles down a giant drain. This tremendous collective clearing event is coming to a close.

The following day brings the Event Horizon. As is typical for me, this significant energy day feels a lot like every other day. The hard work of preparing for this energy event is already over.

I tune into my vision and all I see is a large field of long, brown, muddy grass. This grass has been beaten down by the massive flow of purifying water. Even then, I know instinctively that new growth has already begun. It cannot be seen yet, but it is there. It is already being planned in the roots, in the sun, in the earth. The future of this field is assured.

Over the next few days I see the monocots – the flowering grasses – start to emerge. First, white little tentative nubs appear. These then grow longer, greener and sturdier until the field is a mass of green with swaths of flowers. Each flower so small and lovely, but together they create an incredible field of such beauty!

The cleansing river occurred in "real time", but this field seems to be a preview, a *knowing*, of what is coming. It will take some time to come to fruition, with each person growing and flowering in their own individual way, but it *will* come about in amazing ways.

When reading this segment, The Dragon Heart told me, "I know exactly what the Sewerline is. It is the channel for the release of "Human Egew" – the thick black gunk that humanity's ego-directed harm has created over millennia. This clearing is so necessary and so incredibly timely."

Sewerline Download Experience

It is your time to flower, to grow. Sit or lie back and close your eyes. Open yourself to release all that no longer serves you. Feel it wash away behind your spine. Hold on to nothing. Let it all go. Know that new growth is coming for you in a very beautiful and natural way.

Notes

Notes

Hawaiian Vacation

The lady lying on the table before me takes off her knitted hat, revealing a sparse covering of hair, a sure sign of chemotherapy. As she settles onto the reiki table, she tells me that she has spent her lifetime taking care of her five children – now adults – but now, finally now, she is focusing on taking care of herself.

My lady has dealt with quite a number of serious illnesses over the past few years, but it is cancer that has finally convinced her to change. As she speaks, she stays focused only on the need to take care of herself. I gently introduce the idea of accepting help from others.

"It can be hard to accept help when you've always been the one giving it," I say, "Now it is your turn to receive. Just lay back and relax and we'll get started."

She has no trouble accepting the healing energy as it starts to flow. I am glad to feel this flow and know that my lady has already reached the point where she can easily receive. She truly is ready to give to herself without reservation, allowing others to bring assistance to her.

At her head I immediately see a hibiscus flower and a Hawaiian beach. I can hear the waves lapping at the shore. Around the edges of my vision, palm trees sway in the breeze while little crabs frolic in the grass and sand below the palms. Occasionally, a seagull flies by. I am enjoying a view out over the water, as I listen to the waves.

My lady and I are on vacation. We are basking in the sun with absolutely no worries.

What does this mean?

Simple. It means we are on vacation. With no worries. Basking in the sun. Lots of work is still going on elsewhere, making things ready, but it is not time for us to catch a plane back to the mainland and get started. It is time to for us to rest and relax and absorb the new energy.

This continues until I get to the hand positions at my lady's torso. I start to smell coconut. It is a new sensation, bringing this vacation even nearer.

When I reach her abdomen, something changes.

I watch a closed lotus blossom open up, petal by petal. Only these aren't all flower petals. Some are hands. Hands which unfold, revealing the reiki power symbol on their palms. Once all the petals of this special flower are open, these power symbols become eyes. This seems very solemn and symbolic, but I don't know what it means. Its meaning will be crystal clear for those who have the knowledge.

Her knees are cold bone. They are not going forward, but are focused inward, drawing in the energy. The beach view returns as I continue on with the session. The top of her right foot takes in an abundance of sparkly effervescent energy, while the underside of the foot is rooted into the ground by only a 6" black plastic spike.

I wonder if her left foot will feel the same.

No. This foot draws in the energy firmly, focused intensely on healing an old break, an old sprain.

At the bottoms of her feet, violet eyes appear. They look exactly like the animated eyes on the bottle on the old "I Dream of Jeannie" television show's animated introduction. These eyes look at me, then look far, far past me, searching the distance first to one side, then the other, considering the possibilities. They seem to be searching out a new site to root in, choosing between the old Earth energy, the new Earth, and the next world.

After the session my lady asks if I could feel or sense any of her physical issues. I tell her that I could feel the energy draw differently at different places, but I didn't tell her about the intuitive messages I had received. It didn't seem appropriate or necessary. This is typical for my volunteer work at the Cancer Center.

I did tell her that her left foot seemed to be healing an old injury. She confirms this, as she had had a very bad break and sprain there many years ago.

Hawaiian Vacation Download Experience

This is your vacation. A time to refresh and rejuvenate as you rest and relax. Sit or lie back and let this powerful sense of relaxation overtake you. You have no worries. You are in the perfect place for you right now. Take your time.

Notes

Notes

Any Moment Now

My lady comes dragging in for her session, ready to accept any and all energy. She has been having a rough time this week, feeling very tired from her chemotherapy. We visit just a little bit and get started right away.

I don't know if I will receive any intuitive messages. Lately, working on myself or family members, I haven't been seeing or hearing much of anything. It reminds me of my first months as a reiki practitioner, before I started to intentionally develop my intuitive abilities. I feel the energy flow and sense when to invoke different symbols, but that is all.

This has happened to me before and I know it will happen again. I am grateful for the reminder that the energy flowing to the client is the only thing that is truly needed during a healing session. Intuitive messages are many things - fun, entertaining, meaningful - but they are not required for healing. This reminder keeps my focus on healing and holds my ego in check.

I know that when - and if - my intuitive messages return, it will happen in its own time and its own way. I feel no expectations. No demands. Just acceptance and gratitude.

I place my hands on my lady's wigged head and immediately I hear Deanna Durbin singing! Deanna Durbin was a child and teen star in the 1930's and 1940's, much like Judy Garland. Her movies and soprano voice were so popular she is credited with saving Universal Studios from bankruptcy. Disgusted with the industry as she grew into adulthood, she retired early, moved to France, and was forgotten by modern audiences. Still, I hear her voice singing clearly.

"Any moment now things will start.
Something new stirs my Heart.
Any moment now bells will ring,
Trumpets blow, Angels sing!"

Ah! Any Moment Now from Deanna Durbin's film, Can't Help Singing, one of my favorite films of hers, although it has been many, many years since I last watched it. This song continues singing throughout the entire session. There is a beautiful sense of something wonderful on its way.

As I perform the hand positions for my lady's head, I see a vision of a graveyard. It does not feel scary or ominous in any way. Vapor rises from the graves straight up to the Heavens. This gray vapor transforms as it rises, turning to gold! I immediately know what to do.

At the next hand position, I invoke a personal symbol I was gifted with a number of years ago, Sangre de Cristo. Sangre de Cristo means Blood of Christ. It is a symbol of deep forgiveness for self and others.

As I finish drawing Sangre de Cristo, I see this same grey vapor begin to rise from my lady's body. It, too, turns gold as it ascends to Heaven. Suddenly, both my lady on the table and I simultaneously tilt our heads to the right.

Just then, my lady "wakes up," fearful, thinking I had left the room. She is afraid to be alone.

"I'm still here," I assure her, "I just had my hands under your pillow. Everything is okay. I'm not going anywhere."

She settles back down on the table and we continue the session. I invoke another personal symbol, Luz de Cristo, the Christed Light, to fill the lonely void left by the removal of the dark vapor. (An even more ascended version of this personal symbol is the Luz

Diamonte de Cristo. The Christed Diamond Light. But this is not needed at this time.)

As the session continues and Deanna Durbin keeps singing "Any Moment Now," the energy feels effervescent, almost like champagne bubbles.

"All you did was breathe my name,
Hold my hand
Suddenly the world became
Wonderland!"

At my lady's legs and feet, I get a strong visual of a man trying to enter Disneyland while wearing an inappropriate shirt. He is taken aside and barred from entry. But he isn't just turned away. He is taken aside and counseled.

At first he is angry and belligerent.

"What do you mean I can't get in? I have my rights! I can wear what I want! You can't do this! You're denying my Freedom of Expression!"

The gatekeepers gently ask, "What of all the others who come here? Our first responsibility is to all of the people who come here to escape the ugliness of the world. If we allow your shirt inside, it will jolt people out of the joy and happiness they feel within and remind them of the pain and ugliness of the outer world. Would you deny them their right to pure, lighthearted happiness?"

A light dawns in the man's eyes. He understands. It is something he has never considered before and this new knowledge kindles a light to shine within his soul.

Up until this point, this man has been somewhat representing my lady, but now her role changes. She appears as herself and is treated as a gatekeeper in training.

She is asked, "What is the appropriate treatment for someone who tries to enter a place of joy with an inappropriate shirt or a heart with an ugly message scrawled across it? Should they be banned from ever entering?"

This begins a discussion of different possibilities and my lady is led to consider each one in its many aspects.

"Could he maybe turn his shirt inside out and be let in?" she asks timidly.

"We could do that, but if his heart hasn't also been turned, what is to keep him from changing his shirt back around once he is inside the gates? What does it mean to the Park if we allow this hateful message within, even if it is hidden from view?" the Gate-keepers reply.

"Could we send him away until he comes back with a different shirt? He could go home and change or maybe go buy another shirt at the store."

"That is a possibility. But he may have travelled far to come here and be unable to return home and come back in time. He may not have extra money to buy a new shirt. What then?" the Gate-keepers parry.

"Hmmmm... We could give him a new shirt and let him enter." She suggests.

The merits and shortcomings of this possibility are debated, too. Would he truly embrace the lesson if they gave him a new shirt? Would it encourage others who are not yet ready to enter to wear inappropriate messages just so they could get a free shirt?

When many different options have been fully considered, it is time for my lady to make the final decision for this particular case.

I do not know what her decision ultimately was.

After the session ended, my lady apologized for making a sound near the end.

I hadn't heard her at all.

She explains that she had fallen asleep, but didn't realize it. She thought I was asking her questions and she was answering them. Then she realized that she was dreaming it all.... or so she thinks. But we know different.

Any Moment Now Download Experience

Breathe slowly through your nose, sit or lie back comfortably, and relax. There are lessons here for you. There is energy here for you. Rest and breathe. Allow these lessons, this energy to come to you. It is coming. It is coming. Even if you do not recognize it, it is coming. Any moment now.

Notes

Notes

Human Sacrifice

I am very happy to see this gentleman back again for another reiki appointment at the Cancer Center. It has been about two months since I first saw him for a session. Since that treatment, he tells me, his life has changed so much for the better!

In his fifty years in the world of metaphysics, I am only the second person he has ever trusted to share reiki energy with him. When he first heard about me, he says, he knew I was exactly who he needed to get to the next level in his life.

Since I last saw him, he has worked with his doctors to find effective pain medication to manage his severe health ailments. One of his Spiritual Teachers has stayed at his house for six weeks in what became a transformative experience – AND he announces that he is in a new relationship for the first time in ten years!

He also tells me of a tremendous experience he had recently with a rattlesnake out in Joshua Tree.

He had hiked out a mile or two from pretty much anything and found a place to sit and meditate. As he sat, he became aware of nearby movement and opened his eyes to see a rattlesnake. She wafted back and forth, ambling towards him in her snaky way.

She sat for a time, just enjoying his energy and the peace they shared together, then she zigged and zagged closer and closer until he got the strong impression that she wanted to sit in his lap!

"Oh, no," he said, "That's a little too close," and he moved away a few feet to another spot.

This repeated itself three times before he decided it was time to head back to his car. The rattlesnake never coiled, never shook her rattle, never shied away or became defensive. She just shared an hour with him in peace.

He was truly grateful for what our past energy session had opened up for him.

I begin today's session and soon see my gentleman sitting cross-legged in an Egyptian pyramid, meditating alone in a spacious room. Light streams in to bathe him from many different directions. There is a feeling of deep reverence for what I am witnessing. Then...

In my mind's eye, I see him start to cough violently while convulsions shake him. I open my eyes to peek and am relieved to see his body lying peacefully and still before me. I close my eyes again and take a deep breath.

In my mental vision, he coughs up a four inch long piece of bloody tissue. It is a piece of his heart.

As if this isn't enough, I now see him lying on the floor of the pyramid chamber being sacrificed in some kind of ancient ceremony. Someone in ceremonial robes uses a special knife to slice down my gentleman's centerline. The Being in ceremonial robes reaches his hands down into my gentleman's chest and pulls out his still-beating heart, holding it high.

"Uh," I say in my mind to Spirit, "I'm not sure I should be seeing this. I'm a Love and light person. Hearts and flowers and unicorns. Human sacrifice is not really my thing. This is getting to be too much for me."

"Shhhh!" I see Horus, the falcon-headed Egyptian God, standing next to me at the sidelines, watching intently, and cautioning me to remain silent. It is a privilege to be a witness to this solemn occasion, but it is a privilege I wish I could do without.

With that, a semi-sheer curtain comes down, muting the view for me. I can tell that things are still going on behind the curtain, but I cannot see exactly what. Without the horrific visual, I can relax. I know that whatever is going on back there is important.

I continue to send healing energy steadily and strongly. This does not feel like regular reiki energy at all. It is something new. Something much more powerful and transformative. Then the curtain pulls back.

I see my gentleman's lifeless body lying on the ground, but I cannot see him very clearly. The light shining on him has a shimmering green aspect, as though the pyramid is under water. What I do see looking very clear, even in this watery light, is a *new* him emerging from the wound of his old body. He looks clean and strong and vital.

Now my intuition takes me back to the living body on the reiki table before me. I can sense my gentleman's heart and lungs. They feel so happy and light! So healthy, able to move blood and oxygen easily without the tight constriction of old pains. It is wonderful to sense this strength and resilience, but more than that, I can feel the blood moving healthfully throughout his body. I can feel the peace and agility of his nerves and connective tissues.

My view jumps back to the piece of heart my gentleman coughed up earlier. A falcon and his chicks are feeding on it, tearing off pieces of flesh to devour.

I become aware of small, papery seed pods blowing by. Little thin round pods, with a kernel inside each pod, are blowing out to the world. I pick one up and looked at it more closely. The kernel looks to be red and pulsing... it is a tiny part of my gentleman's living heart tissue going out to the world, spreading Love and human kindness.

I look over and see there are branches full of these seed pods, releasing more and more Love with each moment. Horus was right. It is a privilege to witness this incredible event.

My vision takes me to a vista of hillsides, while my ears hear, "We deal with all the annoying people differently here." All of the hillsides are planted with new corn in the New World. Yes, Spirit confirms, we deal with all the annoying people of the world by transforming them into new unsullied growth.

So often in our spiritual paths we have to be willing to die in order to grow. At least it feels like we're going to die. In reality it is like a snake shedding its skin or a hermit crab moving into a bigger shell. We outgrow the old and have to let it go in order to move into the grander new.

I have experienced this death and growth process personally a number of times over the years, but this is the first time I have ever witnessed it and helped someone through the process with Divine energy. Later I personally feel the effect of those heart-seeds when, in meditation, psychic surgery is performed on my own heart.

"Let's take care of this," the masked surgeon says, "Your heart has slipped out of place. It has detached. See? It should be up here." He raises my heart a few inches and I can feel the difference. With that, he spends a few minutes sewing my heart to the heart wall to anchor it correctly.

"There!" he says when he finishes, "Now your heart is in the right place."

I smile and thank him... and my generous gentleman.

Human Sacrifice Download Experience

It is time to prepare yourself for your current phase of birth, death, and growth. You are safe. I am here with you to aid the Divine in sending you exactly what you need at this period in your growth. There are great leaps ahead for you. You must prepare to greet them. Sit or lie back comfortably. Close your eyes. Allow your experience to come to you, to embrace you, to envelop you. Trust and relax.

Notes

Notes

Only Now. Wake Up! Too Soon.

As I begin this session on my gentleman, the first thing I see is a traditional Japanese woodcut of a man thrusting a very long stick into the ocean. He is intensely concentrated on his task. This image is far off to the left side of my vision.

As I change hand positions, I see a close-up view of the underside of a fly. Soon I realize that the fly is upside down. Is it dead? This is followed by visions of a black beetle, a date beetle, and a cockroach, all belly up and still or very nearly still. Are they dead or dying? I don't know.

Do they represent disease? Death? Poisonous environments? I don't know. I cannot get clarification.

The next vision I see isn't an insect, but what exactly is it? It appears to be a sort of sickly hairless cat or something. Eventually it settles into being a hairless primate fetus which then transforms into a human baby or long-term fetus. But it is too soon, too soon...

A glass bowl appears, filled with water. The baby is gently placed into the bowl and completely submerged in the water. There is a slight greenish tint to the liquid. As I watch, a purplish vortex appears in the water, a mini-tornado reaching down to the baby's hara.

The hara is a person's energy center. It is located about two inches into the body just below the navel and is like an umbilical cord to the Universe. It is where much of our intuition and higher knowledge comes from.

At the next hand position, I can feel the dark inkiness of space with the brightness of stars flowing through my hands, while planets flow from my third eye to the third eye of my gentleman. This glorious healing energy is filling him with new Universes.

The red, papery pods of the Chinese Lantern Plant appear when I move my hands to a new position. I can hear the soft rasp and rattle of the pods brushing against each other in the breeze.

In real life, these pods protect the fruit of the Chinese Lantern Plant, but in my vision, each papery covering opens to reveal a bright red flower with a golden center. Bees appear from out of these golden centers, flying off to spread their pollen, infusing the world with the substance it needs to grow, flower, and fruit.

These fruitful pods quickly dry up and become seed pods to blow away and repeat this process elsewhere, spreading much needed blessings.

As I move to the arms and torso of my gentleman, I am blocked from seeing the depth of the work taking place with the powerful healing energy.

All I can see is a beautiful Japanese painted screen with clusters of the Chinese Lantern Plant's red pods draped decoratively over the corners. But when I reach the upper abdomen of my gentleman, I can see *something*. I just have to figure out what it is.

A mass of knotted intestines tangle purposively to hold my gentleman's inner child in place. It appears as either a fetus or small baby in among the intestines.

My immediate inclination is to use higher level reiki symbols to unknot the intestines and free the inner child, but I know intuitively that my specific purpose in this place and time is to simply send Universal Life energy without judgment or interference.

The lower intestines appear to be hot, red and burning. As I watch I finally understand what the Japanese man in the woodcut I saw at the beginning of the session was doing. His long, probing stick was clearing a way for the ocean waters above to flow down and bring cooling energy to these burning red intestines.

As I witness the bright hot redness cool to a dark red, I am overcome with gratitude for the service the Japanese woodcut man has given to my gentleman. "Aregato, Sensei" I say in my heart as I finish sending energy to the lower intestines and move down to my gentleman's knees. The knees are completely immobile.

Plinth. Monolith. These words repeat over and over. Plinth. Monolith. After the session, I have to look them up to be sure I understand. Plinth. Monolith.

A plinth is the square block a column or statue stands on. It is the lowest part of a base, or the sub base. The basest base of them all. The support of EVERYTHING. A monolith is a single upright block of stone that serves as a pillar or a monument. Typically, a monument of this sort is for religious purposes.

Soon I see a close-up vision of solid rock with moss growing on it and warm water flowing down it. Is this the ocean water that gathered the heat from the lower intestines? Possibly. I am just to watch and accept.

"Only now. Only now." These words keep my focus on the now moment and the vision before me. It is just the granite, the moss, and the water.

At my gentleman's ankles, I see a crowing cock strutting around, "Wake up! Wake up!" his crow sounds loudly. "Wake up!" But except for the light on this rooster, it is dark. There is no glimmer of dawn.

"Too soon. Too soon," comes the response from the ethers to the rooster. Soon both phrases are repeating at once. "Wake up! Too soon. Wake up! Too soon."

Energetically, it is time to hit the snooze button, get a few more minutes of sleep, and be ready to wake up soon.

At my gentleman's right foot, I see the darkness of space, dotted with thousands of stars. I expect to see the same at his left foot, but instead there are sand dunes covering vast stretches of land. I know there is hidden life somewhere, somehow, in all of that barren nothingness, but all I can see is shifting hills of sand.

Suddenly, a lightning strike hits the ground fusing the sand instantly with intense heat, creating a fulgurite. A fulgurite is a form of fused quartz, a special kind of glass created by an intense release of energy. It is a powerful manifestation tool, a powerful cellular healer, and an aid to enlightenment.

At the bottoms of my gentleman's feet, I see swirling red. The color is not too bright and there is a darker, almost brownish, red mixed in.

I see no roots at all, just this swirling redness. I cannot feel or sense any heat at all, but neither do they feel cool. The right foot shows swirling gas and dust in space, while the left foot shows swirling mud.

As I watch the movement, I am given a deep sense of peace and understanding that the energy will teach my gentleman exactly what he needs to know.

Only Now. Wake Up! Too Soon Download Experience

What message, what healing is here for you now? Sit or lie back comfortably. Close your eyes. Breathe slowly and deeply through your nose. You have been feeling a desire to do and be too much, too soon. All is proceeding as it should. Relax and accept the healing that is here for you now. Relax and open yourself to the messages. Relax and let the energy teach you exactly what you need to know right now. Let the energy show you exactly what you need to feel.

ONLY NOW. WAKE UP! TOO SOON.

Notes

Notes

All of This

Things heat up as I initiate this reiki session. Before I receive a single visual image or "spoken" message, I start to burn up. Sweat pours down my face, back, and chest. This energy is fierce. It comes on strong, with a do-or-die intensity, taking no prisoners.

I hold my face back so my sweat won't drip on the young lady lying on the reiki table in front of me. I place my hands very lightly over her eyes with just the heels of my hands touching her eyebrows. I don't want to do a full-touch hand placement while I am so sweaty. I want her to feel comfortable and relaxed.

This is her first reiki session, ever.

After a position or two, a visual comes to me. I see a long, thin snobbish face with a long, thin pencil moustache. The view pulls back and I see that the man I am looking at is head waiter at a fine establishment. He holds a large covered tray aloft, balancing it professionally on one hand.

Is this tray for me or for my lady? I am not sure. He brings the tray over to the round table where my lady and I sit side by side. With a flourish, he raises the cover to reveal different dishes. The only trouble is, I can't see any of them.

They are just blurs to me.

Ah! I understand. It is not for me to choose. These are all selections for my lady to make.

"Oh! They all look so good!" she exclaims as she looks over the different dishes on the tray. She makes her choices.

"This one," she points, "this one.... and.... this... no! *That* one right there!"

The head waiter places her choices on the table, covers the rest and walks away with his tray. I reach over to a plate of some kind of meat and pull it towards me. The head waiter returns to tie an extra large napkin around my lady's neck to act as a bib.

I slice the meat into bite sized pieces and begin to feed my lady, bite by bite. I take a spoon and feed her a few bites of some kind of violet-colored custard. I take a sharp-tined fork and spear a few bites of a chopped green salad for her. It seems important to use each utensil – knife, fork, spoon.

When she has her fill, I reach for a frosted heart-shaped cookie. One half of the heart is red, the other pink. I break the cookie in half and we share it, my lady and I. I think I have the red side and she has the pink, but I can't be sure.

We smile at each other as we eat the cookie, happy to be sharing this new Divine Love energy.

When we finish our cookie, we get up and walk over to a balcony to gaze up at the moonless night sky. We are both wearing long white robes.

"You know, don't you, that all of this," I wave my arm to include the entire night sky, "is inside of you."

She looks questioningly at me for a moment, then, at my nod of assurance, turns back to the night sky and inhales deeply, pulling in everything in sight, sky, stars, planets, until all of it is inside of her. Only a whiteness shows from the balcony view, as far as the eye can see.

It is not a nothingness, yet it isn't a white screen. It simply *is*.

"You know, don't you," I say again, gesturing to the contents of the room, including myself, "that all of this is inside of you."

With her next deep inhalation, she takes in the room and everything in it, including me.

She looks around herself at the whiteness and asks, "Then where am I?"

I answer from deep inside her, my voice sounding like I am deep in a cave, "You are inside yourself as well."

With her next breath, she inhales herself and reappears in the room with me. I receive the dual view of this placement of us both inside of her and of her as a tiny white speck in the field of whiteness beyond us, the whiteness that encompasses the place we had been previously.

The speck of my lady in the whiteness speaks.

"Do you only exist inside of me?"

"No," I answer as another speck of whiteness in the whiteness, "You are inside of me as well."

"How is this possible?"

This question leads us to be created again in physical form, walking side by side in a lush grassy green park.

As we walk, I explain, "The whiteness is God's light, the pure bright light of the Creator. We are all, each of us, a part of that light. But each of us is experiencing life as an individual in human form. The me that is inside of you is me as seen through your eyes, heard through your ears, filtered through your experiences, attitudes, and opinions.

"The you that is inside of me is you as seen through my eyes, heard with my ears, with my own filters of experience and viewpoint in place. It is all valid. It is all real. It is all the truth, even though the same experience, the same people, will be experienced in vastly different ways, according to each experiencer."

We walk on, deep in thought, assimilating this new concept of life and the Universe.

In the reiki room it is now time for me to move on to the next reiki hand position. As I do, I find my energy trying to reach out and sense my lady's cancer. This is unusual for me. As a reiki volunteer, I am given no documentation about the clients I see. Also, many of our clients are staff or former patients and do not have active cancer.

As I send healing energy to the patients I see at the Cancer Center, I generally receive no energetic information on their cancer. For some reason, to me it feels like prying into their personal affairs, like snooping. I also don't want to know their outcome. I want to keep all their possibilities open. So as a rule, I don't actively try to figure out why someone is at the cancer center. But when my intuition leads me somewhere I follow.

I can sense something at my lady's left armpit. I send extra energy there.

At the next hand position, I find my lady and I are still walking in the park, discussing the nature of life and the Universe. It is as if we are discussing a work of classic literature.

As I center in on the conversation, I hear my lady saying, "This conception of life and time creates a narrative problem. What tense do we use for the narration? Past tense? Future tense? Since all things are happening at one singular point in time, did you give me reiki? Am I receiving reiki? Are we about to share reiki? Where are we in time?"

I cannot hear my entire answer, but it starts with this:

"We are spiritual light beings living these current lives as human manifestations in a linear time sequence. So it is true that all of our experiences are happening in a single moment known as NOW. As time-free energy, this is easy to understand. As linear time-frame humans, it progresses from one thing to the next."

"But notice," I continue, "What I just said is already a memory. What is happening to you now, what you are hearing now is all that truly exists. My next words have not happened yet. There is only now. And now. And now.

Even your memories come to you in the now. Even your dreams of the future come to you as now. Now is all there is."

At the next hand position, our discussion continues, but it focuses on a new topic.

"Where are we?" my lady asks, "If I am having my life experiences as a dot of God's light and you are having your experiences as a dot of God's light, how do we come together to have this discussion here or our reiki session back in the "real" world?"

"Ah!" I smile, "Your life energy and life experience is like a bubble that surrounds you and IS you. This is the space into which you inhaled everything earlier. I have my own bubble, my own aura. This time spent together is when our bubbles come together and intersect."

"Every one of these intersections occur when different consciousnesses come together to share an experience. They can happen to different degrees for different people. You and I are intersected equally for this experience, but those people over there," I point over towards a young family playing with their kids at some swings and slides in the distance, "barely touch our bubbles."

"If you are driving and someone cuts you off, they will be very much inside of your bubble as you react by slamming on your brakes and cussing them out, but if they didn't see you and are completely unaware of having caused you momentary harm, you are merely on the edge of their bubble."

"When lots of people gather, there are numerous bubbles intersecting in different ways all at the same time."

"Are people the only things on Earth with these consciousness bubbles?" she asks.

"No. Every living thing has its own bubble."

As I walk, I look down at the grass below our feet.

"Each blade of grass here has its own bubble, every tree. As we walk, our bubbles intersect with the bubbles of the grasses we tread on."

With that, I come to a dead stop, hit with the realization that, just as I have the Universe inside of me, so each and every blade of grass has the Universe inside of it.

I am inside each blade of grass... Wow.

At the next hand position, I hear a panicky, "I'm late! I'm late! I'm late!" over and over again. Using higher level reiki symbols I work to remove this anxiety and to reassure my lady's cells that everything is perfect in God's timing.

Her knees feel kind of spongy and are full of holes with some kind of oil dripping out of them. Again, I use higher level reiki symbols to remove anything that needs to be removed for her greatest good and to fill in the holes with pure, Divine light and Love. An eyedropper appears, replacing the necessary oil in the proper places drop by drop.

At her ankles, I feel moved to use grounding symbols to give her a sense of stability and permanence in space, time, and place. Her right foot needs many high level reiki symbols. I don't know why. I am simply guided to invoke each symbol in turn.

Her left foot shows me a lovely pond with a lotus blossom floating in it and drops of water creating delightfully spreading rings. When I transition to the hand placement at the bottoms of both her feet for the end of the session, I continue to see this beautiful pond with its rings of gentle influence and impact.

It reminds me of a quote from Mother Teresa, now a Saint, that I used both in the interior and on the back cover of my book, Community Reiki: The Reiki Practitioner's Guide to Healing the World, "I alone cannot change the world, but I can cast a stone across the waters to create many ripples."

In my lady's particular case, the ripples created at the bottoms of her feet contain a message felt straight through the heart. A beautiful message of pure peace and tranquility. It is perfect.

All of This Download Experience

There is so much for you to learn, to experience. So much of new thought and new-to-you realities. Get comfortable. Sit or lie back. Close your eyes and breathe slowly through your nose. Sink in. You are making your selections from the tray. Sink in. You are traveling to a place to meet your teacher. Sink in. This learning need not contain words. Sink in. All of this is inside you. All is well.

Notes

Notes

Storytelling

As I began the session on my sweet gentleman, I see a drink and hear the word "Sangria". The word repeats itself many times, but I feel a sense of disconnect.

This drink doesn't look like Sangria. It looks like a Tequila Sunrise, with sunny colors fading from light to dark. It also seems odd and out of place to be seeing an alcoholic drink during a healing session. Too worldly.

Things start to shift. The drink widens and spreads itself out, transforming into a beautiful ridge of sandstone. I wonder if I am looking at Sedona and its breathtaking red rocks.

A face appears. I can only see half of it. White, with a black stripe down its nose, or black, with a white stripe down its nose, I cannot be sure.

I see the image of the edge of a woven basket, Is there a lizard image woven in it? A snake? No. I see a little mouse peeking around the edge of the growing basket. It is a large utilitarian basket, part of a granary in a cliff dwelling. Is this the Anasazi?

Maybe. But it reminds me more of Montezuma's Castle, a National Monument in Arizona, just outside of Sedona. The Sinaugua people were the last to inhabit it, although many more ancient tribes lived there before.

Corn is brought from the basket and prepared for a banquet, along with fish from the nearby river.

I see a close-up view of the back pocket of a pair of Levi's. This view broadens out until I can see the denim-covered legs and booted feet of a Native American rancher or pony rider of great skill. I sense that he is Hopi or Navajo. He has black hair, cropped short, and a red bit of cloth that is either a headband or a bandanna around his neck. I cannot be sure. His shirt is blue with small white dots or flowers on it.

He is searching the chaparral for a lost sheep. Snow is falling, and the young sheep is tired from his struggles, so the rider lays him across the front of his saddle and rides with the young one while herding the rest of the flock back to the ranch. It looks to be the 1930's or 1940's.

At the ranch, the sheep are safely enclosed in their pen. As this rancher takes a hoof pick to scrape mud off of his boots before entering the bunkhouse, he glances up at me and I am told, "There is a story in every piece of mud."

My next vision is of a 40-some year old man with long braids. Cahuilla? Pima? I don't know. I feel very ignorant and unqualified to identify his tribe, his rich and honored culture. I can only see this man from the back, with just a peek at the side of his face.

He is in a cave, mixing pigments in a stone bowl. As he crushes the pigments in his bowl, I see the contents transform into a shifting green flame. As the flames move, they form different figures and animals, sifting through innumerable stories until he chooses one to tell.

He reaches his thick finger into the pot, and begins to dab red paint onto the wall of the cave. As he dabs, he sings in a language I don't know. Ghostly images form along the ceiling.

I look up and see a great Thunderbird flying high in the sky, soaring overhead under a darkening sky filled with roiling clouds. I see a polar bear and her cub standing on a shrinking slab of ice. The man speaks.

I listen carefully, knowing that this is important.

"We are the True People. We are the Human Beings. There are many who live to crush the Earth underfoot, but we True People walk lightly on the Earth.

"There are those who live to command the Earth, to act as slaveholders of her resources. But we Human Beings know that we are stewards, shepherds, caretakers of our Great Mother...."

His voice dies away and the ceiling images resume. I see the Earth from space with a great blanket of dark wool placed over her sky. The Thunderbird wings its way ever higher and higher, until it suddenly forces its way upwards, jabbing holes in the blanket, tearing away scraps of wool.

The people of the Earth watch breathlessly as the Thunderbird does his tremendous work. They break into cheers and rejoice as pure, beautiful light shines through the holes made by the great bird's beak and talons. Life had been hard and terrible in the darkness, with many abominations against the land and the True Human Spirit, but now there is hope.

"Hooray! The people cry, "The Thunderbird has poked holes in the sky so that God can see us again!"

Back in the cave, the man with the long braids and the red shirt is silently bent over. I can see his back heaving with emotion as he tries to hold back his sobs at the memory.

Only... they aren't sobs. He is... he is... he is laughing! Great howling laughs erupt from deep in his belly.

"Hahahahaha!" He laughs, "They think the holes are being poked in the sky so that God can see THEM! Hahahahaha! God already KNOWS all! He never left the People! The holes are so the People can see God's light! God did not forget the People! The People forgot GOD!"

Without a word, the man in the cave demonstrates how to bring the light down with each in-breath, how to show the light at the level of the Earth using his heart, and how to share it with others at each exhalation to dissolve the Darkness. The Darkness made by Man.

As he does this, he paints the story with red ochre on the side of the cave. Simple pictures that say so much to those who know how to read them. He is painting this story to last for eternity. He is painting this story to share.

I watch, and finally have to ask him, "Is this teaching for my gentleman on the reiki table, or is it for me? Who is this message meant for?"

He turns to me and I can see his deeply lined face and long white braids. He is much, much older now than he was when his story began.

He explains. "I am telling you a story." He then gestures with his head towards my gentleman, "I am teaching him storytelling."

My gentleman has always had Shamanic tendencies, but has not chosen to follow them. He has not sought teaching, so the teaching is coming to him. Destiny can be postponed, but not avoided. His destiny is coming and he is being prepared.

Then the teaching takes a different turn.

"The ultimate destiny for all on Earth is death," the ancient one says as calmly as if he were making everyday small talk about the weather.

I listen.

"Death," he instructed, "is a beginning. Too many on Earth have been afraid to begin. When the People understand Man's relationship to the Earth and that to preserve her there must be fewer of us, then it is an honor to die."

After a brief pause, he continues.

"When you come to this knowledge fully in your heart, you will smile at each death, knowing it is a blessing. Our duty is to shine light so people understand and do not fear.

"These deaths are needed to restore balance on the Earth."

The Old Man in the cave tells me that he is glad to be dead. He has had many lives in many tribes. He is Awatchoochie of the Many Nations and he no longer has to live on Earth. He has a new life as a teacher at a higher vibrational level and it is good.

Storytelling Download Experience

There is a story for you. You only have to open yourself and receive it. Sit or lie back comfortably and embrace the energy of this teaching, of this story. It is yours. Awatchoochie or another Ascended Master Teacher whispers in your ear, in your heart, the lesson you most need to know right now for your continued growth. Do not expect this teaching to come in the manner you are used to. It is the energy that teaches you now.

Notes

Notes

I AM Pain

I lay myself down on the reiki table at our local Reiki Circle, ready to receive. I had been experiencing some old pains and old energy blockages and I need help to move past them.

It isn't easy for Healers to ask for healing. Many times I have gone to our Reiki Circles only to share the energy with others, rarely to receive, but this time I state my intention to receive healing energy right out as we each introduce ourselves and state our intentions for this gathering.

Master Earl, leader of this Reiki Circle, is the Reiki Master who first introduced me to reiki. Master Earl stands at my head while the other healers in the room place themselves around me.

And so it begins.

I can feel the reiki energy entering, not through my head or from any place where the practitioners have their hands on or near me, but coming up from the Earth's center and in through my lower spine.

Is my root chakra damaged? Do I have a tear at my Sacral Chakra at my back? Is there a problem there? Is that what I have been feeling?

I let the energy flow. It feels so wonderful.

There is no problem at all.

It is simply not appropriate for my root chakra to be engaged and connected to the Earth at this time. My connection to the Earth is through the back of my sacral chakra. That is all.

I relax further, accepting and allowing, requesting and receiving this energy.

"I AM. I AM. I AM. I AM. I AM. I AM. I AM. I AM. I AM," repeats at my heart level.

Then I get a visual. Something pale and spectral. Something... dead? It looks kind of like a fish face. A dead tilapia from the once-thriving, now-polluted Salton Sea.

The face is white with light tones of aqua, purple and pink. The eyes are deep, dark, and hollow.

But wait. It isn't a fish after all. It is... it is human. A small, curled up body starts to form itself into my vision.

Why am I seeing a dead zombie fish-face little girl?

Then it blinks and I realize it isn't dead.

What is this all about? What am I supposed to do?

I take a deeper breath and relax further, trusting that the image I am receiving is for my greatest good, and that all I have to do is watch and allow.

She reaches out her tiny hand and I hold it in mine. Then I recognize her. Pain.

She is my Pain. From my accident.

I remember the Monster Party exercise from the wonderful book, The Power of Receiving by Amanda Owen and I immediately know what to do.

I have to plan a party for my Pain.

"Excuse me just a moment, I'll be right back," I say to my Pain.

I am back in a flash to take her again by the hand and lead her to the Paradise Pier at Disneyland's California Adventure. (It has been re-done as Pixar Pier, but it was still Paradise Pier in my vision.) We don't need a big party, we just need some quality time together.

We walk around and ride some of the rides. As we do this, I share memories of times we spent together there before. My half-dead zombie fish-face little girl of Pain is silent, watching everything around her with big eyes.

"Remember how this shifting Ferris wheel used to hurt me so much every time the car slipped and swung to a new position? I had to hold myself so stiffly!"

"Oh! This whirling ride! C'mon, Let's go! I used to have to be so careful of my neck on this one!"

I am trying to be cool, but I still end up holding onto the chains of the swing for dear life for fear I will fly off. Pain, meanwhile, is utterly fearless, smiling and starting to laugh just a little.

After the ride I look at her and see that half of her face is starting to gain flesh and color.

As Earl - an incredible intuitive healer with deep insights - works on the back of my neck, I hear him say, "Yes. This throat injury goes very deep. It's had a tremendous effect on you."

Wait a minute.

My neck injury is a THROAT injury? As in Throat Chakra? I had never made that connection before.

No wonder I lost myself in my years of Pain. No wonder I have had such a long struggle to know what I want, to speak my piece and to stand up for myself!

I didn't know! I didn't know! I didn't know! But I know now. And that changes things.

A dark red cherry comes up from my throat to be coughed out. Only it isn't really a cherry. It looks like a round piece of bloody tissue with a stem. Then comes a bloody grape.

Next, an orange – a blood orange to be exact – tries to come up out of my throat, but it doesn't quite make it. I can't release it yet, but at least I know it is there to be worked on, whatever it is.

Back at Paradise Pier, I look at my Pain again. She doesn't look anything like me, but now I recognize her. She isn't my Pain after all. She is my Inner Child. Lost and nearly destroyed by years of pain and inability.

Oh my God! That pale, dead fish is my Inner Child!

We need to talk.

We go to Boudin's and both get soup in a sourdough bowl, then we sit down at a bench outside to eat and get to know each other better.

"I am so sorry," I tell her, looking deeply into her eyes between spoonfuls of broccoli cheese soup. (She has chicken noodle.) "I didn't know how much you suffered. I never realized what you lost of yourself from the accident. I didn't know that the pain ripped you away from me. If I had, I would have reached out to you sooner. I hope you can forgive me."

She looks up at me, spoon poised in the air, and smiles.

"I love you," I say.

"I love you, too," she whispers with a voice that is barely more than a breath of wind.

As we talk, her color gets healthier and healthier until she looks like a normal young girl in a pale brick red dress with little pigtails tied up by the top of her head. She hasn't had any hair in a very long time.

We get ice cream cones at Ghirardelli, then we go back to the rides. We aren't done with our ice cream cones yet and we can't take them on the rides. Together, we decide that since this experience isn't taking place in the "real" world, we can just leave our cones at the table and come back to them anytime we want to.

After a few rides, my Inner Child makes some new friends her age and runs off to play with them and my session at the Reiki Circle comes to a close.

I AM Pain Download Experience

Take courage. Your pain, your fears, are not pain and fear at all. They are neglected parts of your own true beloved self that have forgotten how to be loved. Remind them. Settle yourself comfortably, close your eyes, and take three deep breaths, going deeper and deeper with each breath. Travel to a place you enjoy and meet with the part of you that most needs your Love and attention at this time.

Notes

Notes

Honor the People Who Came Before You

The last few sessions had been so amazingly incredible, I didn't know what to expect when I settled into my chair to start this reiki session with an elderly woman. I certainly didn't expect to see an ice cream cone, but that's what I got. I settled in and let the energy flow.

The ice cream cone I see has all the flavors and colors of spumoni, but instead of being one single spumoni scoop, there are three separate scoops of each of the flavors that create spumoni: chocolate, cherry, and pistachio.

As I watch, the ice cream starts to melt, dripping down the sides of the cone. That disturbs me. I cannot sit there and watch perfectly delicious ice cream go to waste.

I reach for the cone to hand it to my lady, but wait... Is the ice cream for her or for me? I feel into the energy for the answer.

It's for me! I get to eat the ice cream! So I lick at the dribble of ice cream going down one side, then I hand it to my Inner Child so she can lick the drips on the other side of the cone. We trade the cone back and forth, eating ice cream and giggling together.

It is fun, this time with my inner child, but the rest of me is well aware that I am being distracted and kept busy on purpose so my ego will stay out of the session with my elderly woman.

At the next hand position, I see June, or possibly Juno. She looks like a combination of a lovely woman in a stylized Mucha poster blended with June Cleaver, the sweet, iconic pearl-wearing mother from the Leave It To Beaver television show of the 1950's.

Juno is the Roman Goddess of the Lives of Women. The woman I see wears a pale green and white gown with lilies of the valley draped across her shoulders.

"I am coming," she announces.

Before I can ask for more information, June transforms into a fairy with colorful butterfly wings and flies off, repeating as she goes, "I'm coming! I'm coming!" as if someone off in the distance is calling for her.

At one point, however, the butterfly-winged fairy becomes the image of June/Juno again. She looks directly, piercingly, at me and says "I'm coming" with a new and different intonation. June/Juno and the incredible energies she holds are on their way. Does this relate in any way to the month of June? Not necessarily. It is more about an new energy.

At the next hand position, I feel energy flowing smoothly, but it feels pale to me. I had been using the mental and emotional reiki symbol throughout the session, but feeling this paleness, I am tempted to spice it up a little with a few other more advanced reiki symbols and their accompanying energies. Before I can invoke these additional energies I hear a voice. It seems to be Juno, but I cannot be sure. It may be one of my regular Reiki Guides.

"The energy flow is for her, not for you."

Okay, I get it. I let the energy flow as it is.

When I place my hands under my lady's head I see a slim gold circlet lying beneath her skull. It is like a royal base for her head to rest upon.

"Honor the people who came before you," My unseen guide speaks, "They may not be at your level, energy-wise, but they were pioneers and extraordinary beacons at one time. Do not judge them by today. Honor them for their own time, place, and space."

I am overwhelmed by feelings of gratitude. In my mind, I see myself lean forward to kiss my lady's forehead with reverence.

Her face and body suddenly become odd, awkward, and disjointed, like a Picasso rendition of herself. I am guided to use the reiki power symbol.

The reiki energy loses the sense of paleness. It now flows gently and steadily. Oddly, it feels boring, particularly after the intense rush of gratitude that filled me only moments ago. I feel the reiki energy as heavy, running on the outsides of my arms.

My unseen Guide speaks again, explaining to me "This reiki energy used to be very exciting and new for you. It used to feel so strong to you. But now you have grown far beyond that. Still, it is the right level of energy for many people to take in. It is Old Earth energy. That is why you feel it running outside of your arms instead of through them. Do not belittle an energy for being older and less than your current capacity."

I return to myself and my inner child. We are still eating ice cream and laughing. My lady's inner child comes over to join us and I hear music. It is a Pete Townsend song, but with a slight modification.

"Let my Love open the door. Let God's Love open the door." repeats over and over.

As the music plays I see my lady picking strawberries while her toddler son looks on. She has done harder labor in the vast fields before, but now is just working her own garden.

I leave my lady to her gardening and approach a woman administrating at a desk on a dais with gorgeous golden light flowing upwards behind her. This great golden light becomes a giant chandelier. The chandelier is upside down. It shines light UP instead of down. This administrator reviews a pile of documents relating to my lady. She nods approvingly, stamps the documents, and sends them UP.

June/Juno returns to converse with me. "The new energy is delightful," she says, "Everyone will be so happy. They will truly enjoy life."

"Even people experiencing pain and trauma?" I ask.

She replies, "This new energy is available to everyone. It is an energy that can easily be accessed. Simply focus on the higher heart. Anyone can do it. Just go from here to here." She points to her heart-space, then moves a little bit upwards to point to her higher heart.

Suddenly I see a piece of tissue. It is a part of my lady. Is it a tumor? A blood clot? I have no idea. I don't want to see this. It is what will kill her.

I am assured that my lady's death is not imminent, but will come in the fullness of time, as is true for all mortals.

I don't want to know this. But I have to. I know deeply that this is something I have to be open to for my own growth and purpose. It goes far beyond what I am seeing and experiencing now. I see myself eating and digesting and passing this vast information, these deep secrets. I just have to accept them. I don't have to be burdened by them or talk about them. I feel myself releasing the moment of panic, the moment of overwhelm.

I feel myself accepting and relaxing. I do not have to consciously understand it all. I only have to be open to it. With this relaxation comes a greater awareness: My lady is rooted in the Old Earth energies. She will enjoy her life and be ready to move on when it is her time. Already, her higher self is excitedly planning her next life.

Honor the People Who Came Before You Download Experience

You are ready to go deeply into knowledge both known and unknown. You are ready to go into the presence of the Divine Feminine and learn secrets of the New Earth energies. Sit or lie back, breathe slowly through your nose for a few breaths, close your eyes, and surrender yourself to the experience. Be fearless.

Notes

Notes

Choice

This session doesn't begin well.

When I go out to the cancer center waiting room at the right time to get the person for my next appointment, my lady is just beginning to pour herself a cup of coffee.

I smile and greet her, but I forget to mention my name. Either that or in the confusion of her juggling her many items and beverages, neither of us can remember me introducing myself.

"Do you work here?" she asks.

"No, I'm a volunteer," I smile.

"Oh, you just escort people to their appointments. You don't actually do the treatments."

"No, I'm one of the volunteer reiki practitioners." Why didn't I tell her I am an Usui, Karuna, and Holy Fire Reiki Master? Feeling misunderstood, I kick myself for being the reiki practitioner who is so unprofessional she doesn't introduce herself.

My lady has had previous experience with reiki. She worked professionally for many years as a massage therapist and energy worker. To her, I seem like an assistant, not an energy healer such as herself.

As we walk back towards the reiki room, I have to hold her coffee and bottle of water while she fishes in her bags for her ringing cell phone.

The two of us completely block the hall until I can gently guide her to one side as she takes care of her business. She is talking on her phone, but not really getting anywhere.

"Who is this?" she asks, "What is this regarding? I'm sorry, what did you need again?"

We slowly inch closer to the reiki room. Ultimately, she asks the caller to call her back in a few hours.

We go through the reiki program paperwork for her file clumsily. She already knows everything and doesn't need to go over the disclaimer or have anything explained.

She isn't being snobbish, she really DOES know a lot, but this is definitely not the excited conversation I usually experience when two energy workers discover each other.

I feel awkward and uncomfortable.

The session starts, but I have forgotten to set the music to play on the reiki timer app I have on my phone. Background noises from the cancer center seep in.

My hands feel ice cold. Fortunately, my lady has taken me up on the offer of a small towel to cover her eyes and block out the ambient light of the room. I am relieved that she doesn't feel my icy hands on her face. Whew!

I doubt if I will get any visions or messages during this session and am just grateful that I can feel some reiki energy flowing to my lady. I trust and pray that the energy will be exactly what she needs for her perfect healing.

Then, with my eyes closed, I get a visual of that same ice cream cone from my last session! What is it doing here?

I take the ice cream cone and give it to my lady as a gesture of peace and fun. I even "boop" the end of her nose with a dot of chocolate ice cream, trying to get her to smile and relax.

It doesn't work.

I invoke a higher level reiki symbol, one that usually puts people right into a deep state of relaxation in no time at all.

It doesn't work. My lady reaches up and scratches her nose.

Why did the ice cream cone appear? It is still hanging around. It has to represent something more, but what?

I ask for clarification on this and hear a voice giving each ice cream scoop meaning. Ah! The triple scoops stand for Love, Acceptance, and Gratitude.

I take that lesson to heart, and focus less on my discomfort and feelings of inadequacy, and more on feeling Love, Acceptance, and Gratitude in my heart for the lady on the reiki table before me.

My hands start to warm a bit.

As I move my way through the different hand positions, I can feel something... I lean into the feeling and get a visual of pink tissue that has been cut and disturbed.

It is the site of her lumpectomy.

Higher level symbols for removal come to my mind, but there is nothing to remove, or so I think at first. I relax and ask Spirit to guide me.

There it is. Right in front of me. There is no hole in the tissue to show what had been removed. The surrounding tissue has squeezed in to fill it. But there is still the *memory* of the hole and that memory needs to be filled.

I invoke a higher level symbol, a symbol of deep Love and acceptance. In my experience this higher level energy doesn't just fill space with Divine Love, it "un-creates" the space, so there is no sense of lack.

Our energy is at odds, my lady and me. It does not fit. When I get to her feet, I expect to run a river of reiki energy through her to calm down the jangly, spiky energy I feel from her. That is, if I am allowed to. It may be that we are just not compatible and another of the volunteer Reiki Practitioners would be a better fit for her.

Either way, I am prepared to see what I can do near the end of the session to understand why our energies are so disparate and to bring our energies into greater harmony, provided that is for the greatest good.

As I lean into the energy for greater understanding, I hear a very upset voice telling me my lady won't make a choice. It is the voice of one of her Guides. This Guide continues to speak, giving me insight.

Going to a tropical country for a year was a choice she made, but this choice wasn't made from the right place, the right feeling. It wasn't made for the right reasons. It wasn't the right kind of choice – the kind that needs so very much to be made.

Time is up for making those feeling choices, the Guide explains, but my lady has been given an extension.

The Guide's frustration is clear.

He complains, "She isn't using it. She just isn't using it. She is wasting this time, and a lot went into play to make this happen so she could learn her lessons in what is truly important to *her*, apart from outside influences."

My lady will go into the future with no choice made and that is no real future at all. She needs to choose what feelings she wants for her future.

I use the higher level symbol for Knowing Yourself at my lady's feet. As I invoke the symbol, I see her wanting to be a 50's pin-up girl, a sex kitten. Not rude porn, but playfully and innocently erotic. She wants to feel aroused, excited, and attractive.

But there is a conflict.

My lady wants these feelings, but she also believes that being aroused, excited, and attractive is not a legitimate choice for a woman in her late 60's. I assure my lady that it is HER choice of what SHE wants going forward. There are no limitations and there is no judgment.

She makes her choice.

Choice Download Experience

It is your turn to make a final choice of feeling. Seek from your higher heart the sensations that make you feel most like you at your best. You are not too late. You are right on time. Look to your past for the moments, the feelings that have made you feel most alive and combine them. Relax, close your eyes, and try on different feelings until you find the combination that feels right for the future you desire. This can be done consciously or unconsciously, but it must be done. There is no judgment.

Notes

Notes

We are here VOL~UN~TAR~ILY

I had seen this woman many times at the cancer center. Her cancer was a thing of many years past, but even now she came every week or two for reiki healing. Some of the volunteer Reiki Masters felt she was taking unfair advantage of the program, but I was always happy to see her.

We settle in for the session and I place my hands gently over her eyes. Spiky energy flows from the outer margins of my palms. This is odd. Typically, the energy flows from the palm chakras at the center of my palms. As I continue through the hand positions for her head and torso, the energy turns blue and a story unfolds.

I see a Blue Whale struggling in turbulent waters. The whale and I both know he has the ability to hold his breath for an extremely long time. He can easily go deep under the stormy part of the sea, but chooses not to. This is a conscious choice. The Blue Whale is riding out the storm up among the heaving swells and crazy spiky swirling energy.

Why? I wonder. I lean into the energy to gain deeper understanding and a calm, deep voice explains.

"We signed up for this. This is why we are here. This storm of energy, these turbulent waters. We are here VOL-UN-TAR-ILY. Only the strong survive. Those who don't survive the turbulent energy changes will be taken to a place of peace and celebrated for their work. They will be closer to God's pure light."

Ah! I understand. Those who survive these times will continue to aid in the Ascension.

As I continue to a new hand position on my lady, I suddenly find myself sitting in a café across the table from the Blue Whale.

From where I sit, I can smell the Blue Whale's spiced chai latte. It smells delicious.

"I can't drink coffee," the whale explains, "My digestive system can't handle it."

In unspoken words, the Blue Whale shares new knowledge and insights with me as we relax and sit together at the café. What is true for this Blue Whale is also true for Lightworkers and Wayshowers at this crucial time in Ascension evolution:

"Any extra weight you are carrying right now is to help you stay buoyant, so you can't easily slip down into the calm, where you would normally be. You have to adjust to the new energies just like everyone else. This will happen relatively quickly for you, then you'll take on your next task."

"We will be going down deep and bringing some of that calm up with us to help those caught in the turbulence. We will surround ourselves with bubbles of calm and show others how to be calm in the chaos."

It feels very calm sitting there with the Blue Whale, even though I know the turbulent storm and violent energy still exists. We are in the same space as all the turbulence, but at a different vibrational level within that space.

"People love their chaos," the whale explains, "their destructive scenarios. You will point out to them just how few of their fears ever come to pass. And for those terrible situations that do come to pass, the people who experience them will find that they have tremendous capacity to cope and survive." That said, the Blue Whale pays our bill, thanks me for coming, and bids me farewell.

I return to my lady, sensing a strangeness in the energy being channeled through me to her upper abdomen. Purple energy streams from my right hand, while green energy flows out of my left to form a plaid field of energy.

At my lady's lower abdomen, the energy shifts again. Pink energy comes out of my left hand, while the green energy now pours from my right. This energy appears as ribbons that weave back and forth in ever-changing patterns.

At her knees I discover an old man. He feels very weary and tired. "I am tired and want to sit down," he says, so I give him a park bench to sit on. He lays down on the bench and immediately falls asleep.

The knees tell you where to go, but during this time of unsteady energy and constant change, there is no known place to go to. Nothing is familiar. The future is in constant flux. It is an exhausting situation. It is best to accept it and rest.

My lady's ankles are filled with fiery energy. Superhero characters and revving engines fill the space. She and her unique energies are ready to do vigilante work in the dark of night. My lady is a Lightworker who is serving the Ascension.

At her left foot I see yellow baby chickie and pink bunny energy with auras. Her right foot shows me a green flame filing its nails and biding its time. Patience, patience. She is only a baby in the new energies that are coming, that are here. She will do her job and do it well.

At the bottoms of her feet, holy fire flames of various colors bring continued cleansing and sustenance to aid her in her growth and her path of serving at the highest level.

After this session, my lady stopped coming for regular appointments. She had received exactly what she needed to feel whole and prepared.

We are here VOL-UN-TAR-ILY Download Experience

You are here for a purpose. You are here to receive exactly what you need. Sit or lie back and prepare to receive it now. Let the energies weave themselves in and about you. Know that the turbulence you see and feel around you are there, not as a punishment, but as a place of highest honor and service. You are here VOL-UN-TAR-ILY. Let the buoyancy of this moment wrap you in Love, gratitude, and strength.

Notes

A Final Word From The Angel in Her Human Form.

After that last reiki session experience, a white sheet descended over my inner vision and all messages and intuitive insights were taken from me. All communication with my higher home was severed and I was cast out. Every time I tried to meditate or tried to connect, there was nothing. Healing energy still flowed during reiki sessions, but it felt pale and the deeper connection that meant so much to me was completely gone.

I had learned my lessons, so I waited as patiently as I could. This lasted for over a year. I *knew*, as I often *know*, that it was for the best. In my hardest moments, pity would be taken on me and I would be given some slight message, some tiny glimpse, but it was always a hurried message from energy beings and Ascended Masters who were preoccupied with other tasks.

The energy of the Earth was changing. The energy of every single person, of every single thing, was changing. This was done quicker and easier without my interference and involvement. I was under construction, too. I needed to relax and allow the changes within myself. I did the best I could and trusted the best I could. In time, as the white sheet began to thin, I started to see colors, I started to get glimpses. It was exactly like starting over.

It is different now. I am grateful as I learn afresh to navigate and work in these new energies. So far I experience fewer vibrant visions, but have more simple *knowings*. New skills are coming. New skills have come.

Today as I ran with a mask covering my nose and mouth, per the current COVID-19 coronavirus pandemic rules, a guided meditation began to play on my i-pod. A meditation to connect to your higher Guides and Angels. I followed along as best I could while I ran, curious to see what would be revealed by way of connecting within the new energies of Nova Gaia.

I relaxed my muscles while keeping my pace slow and steady. I let my eyes close slightly and my vision blurred a bit. My breath continued to flow in and out under cover of my mask. Once upon a time I would have felt a tingling at my crown and seen light pour into me from above. Once upon a time I would have sent roots into the Earth to ground me. I would have felt spacey and relaxed.

That was in the old energies of a world that no longer exists.

I felt mostly here, in this place, on this planet, but the connection was made and made as strong or even stronger than ever before. The energies weren't pouring down from above, they weren't sinking down below; they were coming in from all around me as I recognized the Godhead, the Source, of the other people in the park. A man passed me, walking in the opposite direction with a small white dog, while maintaining a distance of at least 6 feet apart per the rules. I saw their vibrant life energy give abundant light to me as my energy body gave abundant life to them.

The words of the meditation urged me to go deeper, but what I felt wasn't a deepening, but a widening. The same path to otherworldliness that used to take me to higher realms now took me to an otherworldly plane that exists right here with us.

Source is here.

I felt myself surrounded by many Guides, Angels and Ascended Masters. In the past, I would have risen and these illuminated beings would have descended to a "no-place" where we could meet in the middle of our worlds. This time, however, I wasn't greeted as an acolyte or a student.

I was greeted as an equal.

Angels and Ascended Masters smiled warmly and reached out to shake my hand. Guides came to hug me. The value of our energies matched, each with their own unique frequency, none better, none worse. None higher, none lower. It was a gathering of equals. I was among my own. I am an Angel. I am a Guide. I am an Ascended Master.

As are you.

In this Nova Gaia the Highest Heavens are now here. We have only to open ourselves up, to reach out laterally and accept them into our hearts. There is no need for conscious grounding as Nova Gaia reaches up roots of her own and grounds into and around us, giving of herself and making us aware of her intelligence, her balance, and the needs of herself and her children.

The words of the meditation asked me to bring one Being forward, be it Angel, Guide, or Ascended Master. I allowed for this and a Being stepped forward. Archangel Ezekiel.

I could not remember any particulars about this Archangel and what he stands for. "Ezekiel," my mind thought, "I am working on guidance to the land of the Divine Feminine. Shouldn't I be greeting Ezekielle in her feminine aspect?"

The answer came.

"No. You are still used to Ezekiel in his male aspect. This is a period of transition. It does not happen all at once, but progresses at a natural rate. Look closely and you will see that Ezekiel is already in a state of transition."

I focus on the Archangel and see that it is true. I can see part of him clearly, but the other half of him is blurred and indistinct, in a state of flux. This changing Archangel stands before me. We reach our hands out towards each other and clasp them, simultaneously sending and receiving energy of the highest light.

The message is clear, but the Archangel speaks to ensure there is no mistake.

"Yes. You understand. As you give, you receive. As you receive, you give in an equal exchange. Share your light. Share your Love. Know that we are right here with you, that we are not exalted beings to be feared or set on high. We see the Divine in you and know that you are one of us. We know that you *are* us, as we are you. Source is all there is. Source is Love, gratitude and acceptance. The rest is created through the imaginations of human beings. It is all made up. It is a dream. Now you can all wake up and begin to dream a better dream."

The next part of the guided meditation playing on my i-pod includes an invitation for the Archangel to give me a message to help me on my path.

I eagerly look for clear guidance, but receive only the same message I have been receiving throughout this year: "You don't have to do anything on the physical plane. You are already doing your work for Source subconsciously."

At its end the meditation guides the Archangel to give me a gift. I eagerly open a small wrapped package and a large turquoise peacock emerges from the box in all of his beauty.

I thought once again of the focus of this current work on the emergence of the Divine Feminine and wondered, "Shouldn't this be a smaller brown peahen? Something less showy?" I cast my mind for the message Spirit intended. Ah! A reminder that male energy is a beautiful thing. A reminder to honor both male and female equally, to invite all human beings to participate in the opportunities of Nova Gaia.

There was also a second meaning to this peacock as he moved his impressive tail up and down. One I wouldn't discover until I looked for more information on Archangel Ezekiel. (You'll find that answer in the very last word I write in this chapter just before the Download Experience.)

As I exited the meditation, I didn't have to bring myself slowly back to Earth, as I had never left. I didn't have to feel spaced out and floaty, as I had not gone up. My energies had only stepped a bit to the side.

It is an adjustment to have the highest and holiest energies right here, side by side with us. In time, we will forget the rituals and formality of contact with higher beings and get used to having them appear here with us with just an informal thought or two. That is an important part of Nova Gaia. Our work since 2012 has been successful at bringing Heaven to Earth. We would be fools to wish to go back just so we can keep our outdated procedures for connecting to our highest selves. We have outgrown them. Our highest selves are here.

Later, I remembered to look up Archangel Ezekiel and found everything I needed to know in the very first phrase to catch my eye: Archangel Ezekiel is the Archangel of Transformation.

A Final Word From The Angel Download Experience

Spirit works with you. Spirit knows you. Reach out with your energy and feel the space around you. Let your own mastery guide you. Invite Archangel Ezekiel to aid in your transformation. Explore your sense of self, time, and place in the here and in the not-here. Messages and gifts await you.

Notes

Notes

Act II ~ The Fairie

The Universe Delivers what we Need.
What we do for Others we do for Ourselves.

These are some experiences that have edged themselves into my mind as they led me to have more trust in myself, in Spirit, and in the Universe. That trust has given me the confidence and freedom to go further in my own development than I would ever have thought possible. What I learned from these, and most of my sessions, is that what I do for others, I do for myself as well. When I lift up myself, I do it for all of the world. It is a cycle that keeps me growing in all the different facets of my life.

As you look at the Download Experience of each chapter, let the experience sink in. Feel what message the Mandala has to give you in your life experience that relates to the deeper meaning of each sharing. If you are using the print version of this book and would prefer to see the Mandalas in color, you can find them at https://novagaialove.com/MandalasByTheFairie.html. It is a personal preference only and will not affect their working. These Mandalas are extremely powerful tools that reach far beyond the perceptions of your eyes.

And now your journey continues with...

Experiences of The Fairie in her human form.

The Universe Delivers
what we Need.

What we do for Others
we do for Ourselves.

Spirit Talk

A woman, somewhere in her 40s, is lying on my table. As I use energy to go through her body to light it up and remove the energy blockages the person allows for, I get to the Sacral Chakra. Immediately I see the outline and shadow of a fetus. I know this fetus never was born and the information I receive includes why it did not develop to full term.

Throughout the rest of the session, I know I need to approach this and tell this woman about the energy still holding onto the womb. But how can I approach this intensely private matter without triggering emotional stress for the person? This most definitely is at the forefront of my thoughts as I finish the session.

As the woman comes back into her body and we talk, I tell her about all the other things I saw. I still have no clue how to approach this particular energy.

As our conversation winds down, the Universe delivers the way. My client asks me if there is anything else I saw during the session. So I take a big breath and ask my Guides to give me the words. Out of my mouth comes the question "Have you ever had a pregnancy that did not go full term?"

I listen to myself and, like always when this happens, I am so very grateful for the way I am guided.

She tells me "Yes, 20 years ago." I recommend that she talk to the energy that is still holding onto her womb so both can find more peace.

Spirit Talk Download Experience

Since I first took a leap of faith in asking my Guides to give me the right words in a difficult situation, Spirit has never failed me. I invite you to meditate with this Download Experience to hear the whispers of wisdom that your Spirit Guides, the Angels, your Ancestors, and Ascended Masters have for you.

Notes

Spirit Talk
https://novagaialove.com/MandalasByTheFairie.html

Notes

Listening to Guidance

This is the first Reiki Circle I am participating in as the Master Practitioner. Our Reiki Circles consist of talk, teaching, and checking in before we go to the reiki tables to give and receive the Love of "Universal Life Force" energy.

During the talk section of the circle, I notice this gentleman who is at the edge. He is deeply affected by what he experiences without a container to hold his feelings and emotions.

I invite him to the table early on and we start working.

My own recollection of the session is that there were about 6 practitioners extending their most loving, kind, and compassionate energy to the man. The Angel, who was also part of this particular session when she was a new reiki II practitioner, distinctly remembers there being just three practitioners: Myself, The Angel, and one other woman who had been in The Angel's reiki II class.

Only after we talked about this experience years later, I began to question my own memory of multiple practitioners and have come to the conclusion that it was just three of us in human form and a number of Spirit helpers. I felt the presence of Spirit so intensely it never occurred to me that these additional healers might not have had a physical body.

In any case, the gentleman falls asleep almost immediately after the Energy starts to flow, which is a good indication of how open he is to receive the energy.

About three minutes in, his body starts jerking wildly.

Immediately, the other practitioners present back off a bit and look to me for guidance. I feel a moment of panic and know I have to make a decision on whether to stop or how to continue. In this split second I sense very clearly that we have to continue. I smile at everyone and nod to go on sending the energy.

As I get back into the flow, I recognize that this is an awakening for this person. His own gifts and abilities are coming online with every jerk of his body.

What we are doing feels like using a defibrillator on a person in cardiac arrest. With every single convulsion, electricity is running through him to turn on previously unused energy channels in his system.

Within a year this gentleman became a Reiki Practitioner, himself. To this day he is continuing his journey, using Universal Life Force energy to further himself and others.

As for my own learning and growth, I distinctly remember that everyone kept looking to me for guidance during the initial moment of the gentleman's convulsions, including the unembodied Spirit Healers present. As I integrate The Angel's recollection, I recognize this moment for what it was. My actual initiation as a Reiki Master. My practical Final, so to speak.

Listening to Guidance Energy Experience

As you listen to your own guidance, sink into the Mandala of this chapter to hear, see, and feel what you are being called to live in this lifetime. Where does your own Mastery reside? Take time to listen to the answers.

Listening to Guidance
https://novagaialove.com/MandalasByTheFairie.html

Notes

Energy Cleansing

A unique and new experience happened at another Reiki Circle a few years later. It is a crowded room. We have three tables working at the same time to make sure everyone gets their time on the table for healing.

I invite the Practitioners to flow with where they feel they need to be, starting at one table, then moving to another as they feel guided. There is a lot of movement between the tables, with others sitting and resting or talking among themselves at the chairs in the room.

With so many people at the circle, I usually ask one of the other Masters to roam and watch as people come off the tables after treatment to give them the support they need. On this particular day, there are about 10 Reiki Masters in this very crowded and active room.

Towards the end of the circle, my table is occupied by this one particular man.

The moment we start, I realize he has attachments - energies that form into beings that feed on fear and fear's allies of anger, anxiety and depression. These are emotional and mental distortions that make us feel unloved, unsupported and separated. These energies know the exact buttons to push within a person to keep them unbalanced and out of alignment.

I look up and communicate silently with a friend, another Reiki Master working by my side. Wordlessly, he confirms my realization and we hold the line to get these unwanted energies to move and clear.

I ask Archangel Michael and Ascended Master St. Germain for their help.

Archangel Michael wields the white sword of light and puts a protective white energy bubble around the person with the attachments. St. Germain uses the purple flame to clear and cleanse the man's energy.

When we are done, my friend and I help the very disoriented, sluggish person off the table and sit him down on a chair. I go back to the table, and quietly tell the other Practitioners to make sure they are energetically cleansing themselves thoroughly so they do not keep any of the energies we just dealt with.

My Reiki Master friend is taking care of the man and the rest of us go on to share reiki with the next person.

A minute or so into that share, I hear my friend giving this still-dazzled man a sip of his water which is fully enhanced with Crystal Energy.

And the man coughs.

He coughs out one of these energy attachments and it hits me right in my back, smack in the middle of my heart center.

Have you ever watched a Sci-Fi movie? When two ships fight and one of the ships get hit? Where everything tumbles and falls, the whole ship cranking at the seams.

Well, this is exactly what I feel. As the shield protects the ships in the movies, I know immediately that this energy has not penetrated my protective bubble. But I am shaken to the core.

After pausing a moment to take stock and check myself, I realize I am okay. A little shaky, but all there.

After the circle is finished and I tell a friend what happened, I got mad at myself for placing the man's chair right where the trajectory of that energy ball could go straight towards me.

The next morning I woke up with a number of realizations about what had occurred and I felt complete and total gratitude that the experience happened as it did.

When the man coughed, I knew immediately what happened and what to do. There were maybe two other people in the room with enough experience to handle and work with these entities without fear of them. I have always known how protected I am and I am grateful this experience gave me the best confirmation of this knowledge I could ever ask for.

The back of my heart felt wounded and raw for a good couple of months. When I asked other Practitioners and friends what they saw, they told me they saw a Dragon coming out of my back. This makes sense to me. Though I am The Fairie, I have felt connected to Dragon Energy ever since I can remember.

From everything I understand, the dense entity was shattered as it met with the Dragon energy in my back. To this day I am grateful that it hit me and not some other unsuspecting person at that Reiki Circle.

When my friend gave the man the high frequency crystallized water, the dense entity could no longer exist in the higher vibration that the reiki and the crystals created within the man's body and it violently came out with the cough.

If the entity had stayed in the room, it might have gone back into the man or cruised around to find another possible host. I trust Archangel Michael and St. Germain to have directed this experience in the most perfect way to protect all who were present in the room.

As far as these denser entities go, there are not many remaining on this plane of existence as we move into a new higher vibrational world of being. They attach themselves to the energy fields of people whose lower vibration will allow it, either consciously or unconsciously.

The easiest way to detect these attachments is to be fully conscious of your feelings, triggers and reactions in every moment and to use your Free Will so you do not follow through with the denser trigger reactions of lashing out in thought, word and action. Simply refuse to do the bidding of these attachments and clearly, consciously revoke your permission for these energies to be with and around you.

Energy Cleansing Download Experience

As you take in the Mandala's visual experience, feel the protection and the Love that your Spiritual guidance has for you and your life experience.

Notes

Energy Cleansing
https://novagaialove.com/MandalasByTheFairie.html

Notes

The Arcturians

When I first started to work with Universal Life Force Energy I was part of a community healing circle that served the public out of a doctor's office. Once a month, on a Sunday, all kinds of healers would come to offer their practices to the public. It had been going on for a number of years and was quite popular. Every practitioner was kept busy.

Towards the end of one day, I was working with a Reiki Master and a Sound Healer on a young woman. About halfway through the session, all of a sudden the sound healer changed her tunes...

Her voice becomes louder and she starts talking in an unknown language, sounding like nothing I have ever heard before or since. It felt ancient and sacred. After about a minute, she switches to English.

The sound healer tells the woman on the table that she has a message from the Arcturians, if the woman is willing to work with them. Arcturians are Star Beings from the Planet Arcturus. Many myths and legends talk about their healing powers.

The young woman agrees and for about five minutes the sound healer sings in the same ancient melodic and strange tongue she spoke before. There is another five minutes of silence before the session ends. Throughout this entire time, both my Reiki Master friend and I just hold space.

Such a deep feeling of reverence surrounds the entire table.

After this powerful healing, it takes the young woman a couple of hours to ground back. Since the Healing Circle was closing, I hung out with her in a nearby coffee shop until she felt fit to drive home. To this day, we occasionally talk.

The Arcturians Download Experience

Take in the visual component of this experience and feel the vastness of the Universe. Feel it teeming with life, with Love, with abundance and light.

Notes

The Arcturians
https://novagaialove.com/MandalasByTheFairie.html

Notes

Breaking Open

While living in the Bay Area in California I was part of another community healing circle that met on a weekly basis. One of those nights, the circle is already in full swing when the door opens and a newcomer enters. It is a young woman in her 20s, asking with a small voice whether it is ok to come in and join the circle.

She is welcomed with open arms and right away one of the tables is opened to her. I am working at another table with other practitioners, but I can hear this young woman talking. She has recently gone through a suicide attempt, she says, and reiki saved her life.

Toward the end of the circle, a friend of mine and I are idle so we decide to offer this young woman some extra energy. She accepts humbly and gets on our table where we work to stabilize her energy field further. As we end the circle and say good night to each other, this young lady asks for a recommendation for a hotel for the night.

As she is getting advice, my guides prompt me to invite her to spend the night in my living space. I lived in a big house with an extra unused bedroom and none of my roommates were present at the moment. She accepts.

Instantly, I am taken aback and a little scared of what I just did. My brain reminds me that this woman was suicidal and I am taking on the responsibility of getting her through the night. What am I thinking?

On our way home, my healer friend invites us to have dinner at her home and both the young lady and I accept. My friend's house is full of beautiful sacred items and lots of crystals are scattered on every surface available.

So we make dinner and sit down to eat, having a good time, with great conversation and lots of laughter. These are good omens that make me feel better about my decision. Toward the end of dinner, the young woman looks at one of the crystals on the table and my friend invites her to pick it up and play with it.

In an instant, the world changes for all of us.

The moment this young woman holds the crystal, she starts to channel. Words flow from her mouth. She tells us about ourselves, our pasts, our futures, about the world, about the Universe. It is the first time I ever see someone open up like this, but my healer friend has seen it before. She is able to guide the young woman through her first few hours of having the Universe speak through her with profound visions and wisdom.

As I found out later, the young woman did not know anything about channeling before that night. After we got to my house, this young woman ended up channeling for me all night long.

The two of us sit in my kitchen and she plays with every crystal she can find. Towards early morning she falls into a troubled sleep. I stay with her and hold her, soothing her like a mother would a sick baby.

The woman's original plan was to fly out of the area the day after we met. She ended up staying with me for three whole days, being unable to care for her physical body very much during that time. She remains fully connected to the Universe and channels for everyone we meet over these three days. When she is finally stable enough to take care of herself, I take her to her rental car, make sure she is all settled and has her boarding pass to take her flight home out of the country.

For rhe first two years after this experience, I heard from this young woman once a year, but I have heard nothing since. Her email address is not active any longer and I only know her first name and the country she is from. I often think of her, an Angel who got sent to us to strengthen our beliefs and confirm the reality of Spirit in a big way.

Breaking Open Download Experience

We all have the ability to open up to all the wisdom of the Universe. Trust the connection, trust the wealth of information that the Universe holds and wants to bring into this earthly realm through you.

Breaking Open
https://novagaialove.com/MandalasByTheFairie.html

Notes

Spontaneous Channeling

One of the teachings I received from the channeling woman came in very handy later that same year as I was working with a festival doing Harm Reduction. In Harm Reduction we help people through difficult personal moments as peers to help them regain their grounding, perspective, and balance.

On this particular day I came to work in a big tent filled mostly with sleeping, exhausted people. The person I replaced told me about this one man who was suspected of having an extensive psychedelic experience that had already lasted for about a day. He was restless and very talkative.

As I settle in, checking on each of our mostly asleep guests, I hear this man talk. And it strikes me that what he talks about is highly spiritual. So I keep listening.

After some time, one of the other guests wakes up and starts to cry. I found out later that she just had a traumatic experience that she is sorting through. What struck me, though, was how the talkative man reacted.

The waking guest is crying, not saying anything, but my man here has a full blown conversation with her. He gives her comfort in a very detailed way. Soon she started answering and I was able to hear both sides of the conversation. It is advice that the man has for the other guest, and it is very wise, valuable guidance.

For a moment I thought they must know each other really well. It turns out they had never seen each other before.

After looking at all my facts, I realize that this man is channeling and is lost within his own mind. All his Guides are talking to him at the same time and he is simply overwhelmed. So I remember my healer friend from a few months back and how she had talked to the young woman.

The moment I talk to my guest from the perspective of him channeling, everything clears up. His answers are now direct and coherent. He willingly follows my instruction and things get clearer and clearer as he sorts out the many voices in his head and is able to differentiate the many connections to his Spirit Guides as they talk through him.

He soon begins to find his way back to himself.

At one point I doubt myself as he starts to talk about Sweden. Out of the blue, in mid-sentence, he switches over to talk about Ikea and Stockholm. That seems odd.

Could I have been mistaken? Was I wrong to think he was channeling? A few minutes later, someone brings in another guest. A middle aged woman who happens to be Swedish.

The man finally falls asleep for a time. Afterwards he was able to find some ground and presence in our shared reality. I gave him some tips on how to go forward from here; to look for energy healers who know about channeling in his area (he was from somewhere in the Midwest of the U.S.) and learn about his gift.

I think of him often and hope he found his way to fully integrate all he is.

Spontaneous Channeling Download Experience

As you open up to this visual experience, feel your own gifts and talents, your own brilliance, possibilities and transcendence.

Spontaneous Channeling
https://novagaialove.com/MandalasByTheFairie.html

Notes

Harm Reduction

Working at different festivals doing Harm Reduction is a very rewarding part of my life. Meeting someone in distress with kindness, openness, and compassion instead of punishment has given me a lot of interesting lessons about how Spirit works.

From the young man who did not want to be touched and was heavily leaning on me for three hours on a cold, rainy night (I ended up leaving him by a sacred fire in the care of the fire tender), to fighting off heavy-handed security guards who held down a big man who had broken down crying and just wanted to go home, I have been gifted with so many memories and lessons about human behavior in raw situations.

Some make me cry, some make me smile, some make me cringe. All expand me.

One particularly memorable story spans time and space.

I am at a festival in California, when one really early morning I get woken up by a colleague. They need my skills with a young woman who is acting erratically and is waking up her whole neighborhood.

As I get there and engage with her, I realize very quickly that this woman has a personality disorder. She switches between personalities faster that anyone can keep up with. All of these personalities are looking for a very specific crystal that they are unable to locate.

I have no idea where it all comes from, but somehow I get her attention and engage her willingness to listen. Within fifteen minutes she is present and unified within. Five more minutes and together we find what she was looking for. We talk a little more and I leave her with some friends who come by to check on her.

Four months later I am sitting in another place, another State, tending to some people as a young woman walks into the room. She looks familiar, but I don't really know where to place her.

There are three people in the room clearly marked as being available to help others, but she walks straight up to me and starts talking. I invite her to sit down. As she talks about herself and how she keeps herself sane and together, I realize it is my Multiple Personality woman from the festival in California.

She tells me how much better she is doing and how she works with all her personalities to unite into one complete person.

I am amazed at how matter of factly she speaks about herself, how she deals with being uncomfortable and how much more whole she sounds. She never lets on whether or not she recognizes me from the time before and I do not remind her either.

It is all as it should be. She is healing and growing.

Harm Reduction Download Experience

As you sink into the visual component of this experience, think about the "coincidences", the synchronicities of your own life. Feel how they have aligned so perfectly to bring you to this perfect moment.

Harm Reduction
https://novagaialove.com/MandalasByTheFairie.html

Notes

Bigger Lessons

I offer reiki sessions at Crystal Fantasy, a metaphysical store in Palm Springs, CA. It was during winter, around New Years on a Sunday afternoon. A man comes into the reiki room and asks me a number of questions. He is interested in a session but not sure about it. He finally decides he wants one and informs me that this is his first ever session and he is curious.

The moment I touch the man's head, I see myself sitting in a light-filled, airy room, as a child, around five or six years old. I immediately recognize that the man who is receiving reiki on my table is my teacher. He is teaching me and other children of varying ages how to work with the flow of energy.

Up to that day, whenever I encountered an energy blockage in a person I just would push through it. Basically using metaphysical muscle, I just pushed until the blockage opened.

That is what I do when I encounter a blockage in the man's energy system. I am met with a loud, clear and amused voice chiding me, "You know better than that."

Throughout the reiki treatment, this man guides and teaches me to use a very different and much more effective way to work with blockages.

Instead of pushing hard and using strength, he asks me to soften. He talks me through it all, explaining that opening a blockage with might will only get the passage to open as long as the pressure holds. The energy channel inside the body will close again once the session is over.

By softening and focusing on Love, affirmation and compassionate kindness, the body feels safe to open and relax, giving it a much better chance to heal and strengthen.

This session changed my whole approach to Energy. My experience is that the softer and gentler I become, the faster blockages turn into flow.

The man gets up from the table after the session, and tells me that now he is even more intrigued. He was visiting from another country. My hope for the Energy World is that this gifted man will learn more and become a practitioner again on Earth.

He was an excellent teacher and mentor.

Bigger Lessons Download Experience

Let the visual experience guide you into the deeper connections within yourself. The deeper truths that bring forth the freedom of being you in your most brilliant expression and purpose.

Notes

Bigger Lessons
https://novagaialove.com/MandalasByTheFairie.html

Notes

A Final Word from The Fairie in Her Human Form

What you do for others, you do for yourself.

This mantra has guided me through all of my lessons from Spirit and the Energies.

In 2012, in a moment of great personal upheaval, one of my Spirit Guides told me to keep growing and to keep glowing. It was the first direct, clear message that came through from Spirit to me that I allowed for and recognized as such. I *knew* the instant I heard it and I took it to heart.

Learning how deeply growing and glowing go together was a revelation that came later. As I allowed myself to learn through everything I encountered, everything I experienced, everything I heard, everything I saw, felt, and perceived in any way, my life started to make sense.

As I let Spirit flow and surrendered to my truth, it opened my heart, my mind, my soul, and my life. It led to a deeper understanding of what it is to forgive, to be kind, and to be compassionate.

As I was thinking and learning I helped others on their way towards greater wholeness, health, and healing. The Universe made it abundantly clear that all the advice, encouragement and guidance I could give others was meant for me as well. As I applied what I told my clients to my own life, I got a clear sense of who I was and who I wanted to be.

Taking that knowledge and using it to grow as a person has given me more than I could ever give.

Such is the beauty of the Quantum World we are entering. Nova Gaia Love Energy is the Guide into this coherent, loving, kind and compassionate world of togetherness, respect, and unity–this time of Resonance, with Yourself and with the Universe.

Together, we each can achieve our brightest, most joyful expression and create the brightest, shiniest, most colorful tapestry of life for all.

What colors will you add?

A Final Word from the Fairie Download Experience

Close your eyes and create your own mandala. See the colors that come to dance before you. What do they represent? What do they say to you? Dance with these colors and see what you add to this beautiful dance of life.

Notes

Act III - The Dragon Heart

Hello, new friends, I would like to take a moment to introduce myself, I am The Dragon Heart, part of the Ancient One. As The Dragon Heart, I would like to offer an upgrade for your personal journey, an unconditional never-ending comprehendible feeling for every individual to have for the rest of their Earth Walk. A Universal Gift that will keep giving, expanding for eternity.

What is this Universal Gift or upgrade I speak of?

Using the American educational system as a metaphor for life, one starts in preschool. Preschool is like a heaven where one goes to choose their own life on Earth. Before one gets to go to kindergarten – before one enters into Earth – the soul's memories are wiped away. There is a clean slate for new experiences.

Then one works their way through learning and finding joy in grade school. With that understanding, this chapter of The Dragon Heart is about going back to the university to finish one's Doctorate. Some of you may even skip the Masters requirements since the rules on this planet have changed because of the Age of Aquarius. This is your history lesson.

Please note, I am **not** *the one giving the degrees and doctrines; they simply are. They are from the Beings of Conscious Light, where ALL's souls (All souls of ALL THAT IS) and all life forces come from, even beings like Aliens. I am just feeding one what one is looking for. Knowledge once hidden now comes to light, freely given for your consumption. You have thirsted for this. You have hungered for this.*

This Universal Gift is food for thought, information and feeling for the individual, a choice to use or not. Once one opens their heart to the information, one will forever grow with ALL (pronounced in the back of one's throat. It sounds like the AW at the start of the OM sound).

In my truest angelic state, The Dragon Heart, my light body
reaches longer than ALL the Universes combined.
I am wider and deeper than anything known to existence,
I am part of what holds the Womb space.
I am a thread that holds ALL the colors and vibrations of ALL,
of everything that is and is not.

What could be considered scales or horns
coming out of my form like vertebrae
reach their own eternal dimensions.
My form could be compared to steel beams inside buildings,
part of the foundation, the frame
holding the structure together.

I can be seen as a pillar so large in scale
In human form one would only see my crown burning
with more intense Love than a fading sun.
I am pure LOVE
Energy that defines space
the place between dimensions is where one can find my breath.
My sound is the same as ALL, Om

And now we begin...
To Remember...
Truth...

And now your journey continues with...

Lessons of The Dragon Heart for your human form

As It Was

All beings, all material structures, everything comes from one Source. The Infinity of the Source just is. It is not a battery that needs to be charged, nor is it made of machine parts. It has no judgment. It has no end. It has no beginning. It needs nothing. *ALL* is everything.

It is *ALL.*

ALL is Love – first Sung out in the Vibration of the Om – A Love vibration that sings still today!

I can remember an existence that was a warm fuzzy bright feeling. It was before time or space; it was a perfect Humm or the ultimate vibration of oneness. In this existence – before Universes existed, a time before planets, stars, asteroids, black holes, a place where only The Void or Love herself existed – was the phase when there was only *ALL*. When we were *ALL*. When *ALL* was one with the Divine Feminine and the Divine Masculine, only *ALL*.

This One, this *ALL* was how It was for a time unknown. This One, this *ALL* will be how It becomes.

BANG!

Then a thought came to *ALL*. A consciousness, an awareness of its surroundings. The first true self-awareness happened and understanding what *ALL* was and is. This is when *ALL* first split the conscious light from the compassionate void. This was the first dimension ever created. One circle of conscious awareness. The first Wheel was formed.

This first conscious thought was with *ALL* and *ALL*. *ALL* understood everything, yet began to define Its surroundings. The first part of the definition was defining a small circular space. This is the first conscious thought. When "She Who Has No Name", also known as Void or Creation, circled around the Conscious Light, it began to define itself.

In that same moment a linear circle formed and separated *ALL* from *ALL.* A separation, a division, a definition, a conscious creation of a line around itself, surrounding *ALL* within *ALL.* Within an instant it replicated the first Circle of *ALL.*

ALL duplicated Its first conscious thought and slid out to form the Vesica Piscis of two circles overlapping. This is the moment of the whole creation –

Within the Vesica Piscis area, where these two circles overlap each other, another new Creation began to manifest through the vibration of sound and light. Instantaneously *ALL* created Space, Vibration, and Matter.

It is within this mirrored crescent of the Vesica Piscis where the entirety of life was created. It was Divine & Glorious! The second dimension was now in existence.

From this instant as a subatomic particle, *Conscious Light* replicated the circle five more times creating the first Pattern of Life. This is the Sacred Geometry of life. This is where everything comes from, the Vesica Piscis from the 2, into the Seed of Life. This pattern will explode into the Egg of Life.

In less than a millisecond and smaller than an atom, Life was created! Within these tiny molecules of this first thought, this first consciousness came, the first Original Creator beings of every Universe, of everything.

The center being is *ALL*'s Conscious Light and the first circle out was before sound was created. This first circle duplicated the Original Creator Being; *She With No Name* came out and became Dark Matter or Space. It was *ALL*'s Consciousness at the beginning of creation as the division continued; the next circle brought the vibration of Consciousness, Om, the next Original Creator Being. More circles came in quickly bringing the light of Consciousness, the Mer, the next circle was the Ka, the Spirit, and then Ba brought the physical body or the material worlds. The final circle to complete the process is known as ע or Compassion/Love. Now the pattern was complete.

The first Seed of Life created everything from time and space, Universes and dimensions, to life as one knows it on Earth. All material flows from this Egg of Life pattern.

The Original Creator beings expanded out like a flash of light, even faster than light at Tachyon speed! In one instant it went from nothing to everything. The explosion through time and space was like none other. As one flows through the Universe one can still feel this expansion as unlimited possibilities.

It was truly a Big Bang!! It was one incredible BOOM – a boom that exploded, that created multiple Dimensions, various Planes, parallel Universes and more types of life than exists on planet

Earth, more than one can even comprehend. The Third dimension came into existence.

Everything came from *ALL* and everything shall return to *ALL*.

The Void (She Who has No Name) is an entity also known as the Divine Temples. She is the fabric that holds together everything: All dimensions in all planes, all parallel Universes. As she lifts her glorious skirt one can see how the dimensions are just layers and layers of her petticoat. I, The Dragon Heart, am a gathering at the waist of her petticoat, holding Stars and Universe in perfect alignment. Like tulle, layer upon layer making up the parallel Universes that Einstein spoke of. So intensely complex, yet layered so elegantly and full of grace.

She Who has No Name, she is Space but it is an understanding that Terrestrials have not fully comprehended yet. Often in science she is called Dark Matter. Science teaches void is only void of sound or of light or a vibration. Void is not negative. Void is part of *ALL*. The Goddess Void (She Who Has No Name, an Original Creator Being) has many channels and many divisions (dimensions). One can see into her soul through black holes. Black holes are lenses into Dark Matter, or peepholes into unlimited color vibrations. One can feel her between one's breath – she is within one.

Void is the Mother. Void is Shekinah, the Crowned One. Void is the womb of *ALL*'s creation. Void is where stars are born. Within Dark Matter (or the Void) is where stars transition back to *ALL*. The stars in *ALL*'s Universes are the originating points of every Soul in *ALL* of the Universes. The star is the physical form of your soul in its entirety.

I know the Divine Temples very well and have played in her layers. She is not dark, void of light or speechless. Instead she is every prismatic color and every sound that exists or not. She is more like opalescence, sparkling with creation so unlimited one can't even conceive of her. Colors that can't be seen by the naked eye emulate patterns that make Sacred Geometry boring. She is the Love holding *ALL* together.

This great Creator Being, She Who Has No Name, has many deities or understudies, like the Dominions and forces like gravity, to support her immense system and help explain how she works. Space is just there to support the planets, to support the sound, and to support the light traveling. Space is not just void areas, but Space is one's support system as well as the space for creation. Inside every cell of one's body is Void or She Who Has No Name. She is Love, therefore one's avatar, one's very embodiment and personification, is made of Love.

Every star bears a soul from *ALL* – it is called The Godspark, the portion of *ALL* that resides in each creation. Ka, one of the original creator beings, is the conduit of the Godspark. Ka is the Spirit of the Godspark, linking each creation through a golden cord to its star.

When a star dies, a soul has completed its conscious journey and returns back to *ALL*. There are over a trillion suns or stars throughout *ALL*'s Universes and dimensions and they all have a Godspark that carries a soul for *ALL*. Like raindrops, each is a piece of the water of life, each is part of *ALL* burning for the Compassion of *ALL*. Think of *ALL* as living water, a source that flows unlimited. *ALL* is conscious knowledge of Love with no judgment. The Godspark of all Terrestrials are simply droplets of *ALL*.

Each and every star in the sky has a soul attached to it which is directly linked to *ALL* through the Godspark. As one continues to think of *ALL* as a giant pool of Love energy creation goo. It is the goo one sees building up to become a star. When a star or sun is born, when it begins to make its own light and expands, this is the moment when a new soul is created. Ka is the conduit or the way the Godspark travels.

As She with No Name, or Love, creates "space" by bringing the Void, this allows the Light Beings to begin to travel through her. The Light Beings have a Consciousness that is connected directly to the Source or to *ALL*. They are the first creations. The Beings of Conscious Light were the first complete entities created in the instant snap of *ALL* creation. They are *ALL*, as we are *ALL*.

As It Was Download Experience

Close your eyes and let your mind wander. Feel this history. See this history. Explore this history.

Notes

Beings of Conscious Light

Although I am speaking here in my form as The Dragon Heart, one would say I reside in the 1st Order of Beings of Conscious Light, or what humans call Angels. As the Original Creator Beings began to set up and create far more than one can imagine, *ALL* went on its way, creating beings that would carry *ALL*'s communications to its massive creations to help each of *ALL*'s creatures expand with *ALL*'s Will. *ALL* was full of so much conscious Love energy, the angelic realms exploded out with Love by creating the first golden rainbow of pure conscious light in the form of an Angelic Dragon and Mikkel was born.

Beings of Conscious Light are not just of one type. Like humans they wear "different hats" or have different job titles. The same person can be a Father, a Son, a Cook, an Uncle, a Grandfather, a Doctor, a Janitor, an Athlete and a Lover. The Orders are categories to help humans understand the different stages of creation and how everything truly flows together. Like different names describing a person, angels have different levels or forms as well. Each has an area of expertise that *ALL* gave them. For example, Réal is an ancient Dragon lineage known as Raphael. Archangel Raphael is known as the world's greatest healer in Earth's major religions. Guardian Angel Raphael aids millions of Terrestrials in the now.

I emerged from the Angelic Order of the Seraphim: Réal (Rayel) as one of the original seeds of *ALL*. Whereas *ALL* created *ALL*, each aspect of *ALL* is also a creator.

If there were a hierarchy with Beings of Conscious Light (hierarchy only exists for human understanding) it would be said that the Seraphim are the closest to *ALL*, or the first in Order and in the highest choir of *ALL*. They were created directly out of the heart of the *ALL* - *directly out of the heart* of *ALL* - as the messengers, as communicators. Beings of Conscious Light, from Dragons to Angels, are the eyes and ears for *ALL*. They work directly through Ka (The Spirit), like conscious brain waves of *ALL*. To explain it in human terms, all of life comes through this Love.

ALL was so excited to expand out and experience everything that has ever existed and ever will exist. *ALL* created the Seraphim to provide communication with and from *ALL*, since direct communication with *ALL*, itself, is too much for anyone or anything. When one is in the presence of *ALL*, one is immediately brought back into the Oneness of everything *ALL*. Instantly, *ALL* brings one back into the fold.

At this present time in our development, when one wants to communicate with *ALL*, we must communicate through an intermediary. Unfortunately, humans can't communicate at the level of *ALL* yet, for we would be immediately reabsorbed into *ALL* and cease to exist as humans. For now, our human healing requests are delivered to *ALL* through prayers to Ultraterrestrials or the Beings of Conscious Light. The Seraphim act as the highest level intermediaries for our communications with *ALL*.

One can get close to the Source (or *ALL)*. As humans, one's soul is part of *ALL*. Through meditation one begins to feel *ALL* within one's physical body. As one finds higher level balance from within, possibilities become endless.

As The Dragon Heart, I work directly with the Cherubim Angelic Order, where most of the Angelic Dragons convene. Many are Keepers, like vibrant cabinet files stretching out to help hold the space for the Akashic Records. Here is where *ALL*'s conscious knowledge is stored. Here is where one travels to clear out past and future karma for a magical *now*.

At one point in Dragon state, we Angelic Dragons could "stretch" out and make comets. Imagine the state of dancing, exploding into forms of movement within the vibrating, gyrating, joyous state of glorious Love of eternal life! From this greatest and purest form, as Beings of Light we can ascend well up into the hem of the dimensions of the Guardian Angels and care for every individual on the planet. One Dragon has the ability to form a billion Guardian Angels!

The most famous Dragon is found at the Vesica Piscis in the birth of Archangel Michael in Western Culture. In Eastern Culture, the Lung or Dragon was held by the Emperors as symbols of esoteric powers, knowledge, and wealth. Remnants of us Dragons can still be found on Earth for those with the eyes to see. Dragons are real and we have returned to aid the planet once again.

As the Seraphim needed more help with *ALL*'s creation, they expanded out into the Cherubim order and then into the Thrones, as the Highest Love Choir. All of these Angelic Orders worked with *ALL* to create a foundation for the beings that were in physical form. This is how planets and stars began taking shape. The First Order began to line up everything within She Who Has No Name, everything birthed from crystalline Dark Matter.

ALL had already created the first full order of Angels. As humans, we know them as the Seraphim, the Cherubim, and the Thrones. All of these entities work for *ALL*. They are part of *ALL*'s consciousness. They are here to aid in getting the information of *ALL* to all beings in creation. The first Order of Angels also ensure that the souls of the stars are going into each of the beings that flow out as life.

The Cherubim are the guards of our Godspark, they guard the Suns (our souls) and the Akashic Records (the individual records of every soul). They are often seen as burning bushes or as if they are on fire because they burn for the Compassion and Love of *ALL*. They hold the universal wisdom and keep all beings in divine order. The Spirit or Ka, often called the Holy Spirit and the St. Germain Light, became One with the Beings of Conscious Light. This is the Spirit's Soul.

The creation of the Akashic Records is neither the end nor the beginning. This is *ALL*'s library where the Cherubim connect *ALL* to every physical being in all of the Universes. Instantly, the Light Beings set up a system to record the lives of All creation, from the second the umbilical cord is cut or the being is hatched. The Akashic Records have become a university all beings attend in order to understand why and how things are the way they are at any moment in the various dimensions or parallel Universes.

The Thrones are also known as the Wheels as they keep the cycles moving forward. I, The Dragon Heart, can also be considered a spoke in the Wheel of the Thrones. The Thrones order is the mechanism or wheel that keeps *ALL*'s life in motion. Anything of the physical realms, dimensions, or realities – however one understands a physical material place.

Like the Medicine Wheel of indigenous peoples, the Thrones work with *ALL*. They work directly with the Cherubim, as they are Karma or Spiritual Justice. Since the Cherubim have the Akashic Records and keep them as *ALL*'s memories, the Thrones work with the full wisdom and knowledge of the records in concert with each individual soul, so that each soul may achieve all of its incarnations to complete the full cycle of its individual Wheel of Life. Each soul needs to experience *everything*. Every individual soul or Sun must experience life as each of the thirteen archetypes and complete its lessons in order to become One again. There are no time limits for this, no order or specific way to complete each archetype. It is an individual journey of creation and experience.

The Orders are grouped together in three sections, simply because that is the definition the humans found easiest to understand. The Highest Love Choir, including the first three Orders as mentioned above, is comprised of those who are the closest to Source or *ALL*. Not because we are older or better – no we are just in *ALL*'s exact form of pure LOVE Energy. There is no physical matter as humans can understand. That is why most stay in Dragon state up here, without descending in vibration to gain physical form.

The next group or Middle Love Choir of the next three Orders (4th through 6th) systemize the physical or matter. Here is where I get to my purpose of being a space holder. I help in defining the Womb, or what you call Outer Space. We Beings of Conscious Light are not seen as such, but are known in inspirational Zen, songs, art, and the energy of sexual activities.

The 4th Order is the Dominions, who have very little to do with human life – only that they hold the space for it to exist. I flow with the Original Seeds of Life as the foundation of the Dominions' Angelic Order. I am part of the systems that one would never see or fully understand.

ALL created the second realm of Light Beings to help control what was going on in the physical plane, to provide a foundation or a structure for what was being created. *ALL* created the Dominions, the Virtues and the Powers to work directly with Dark Matter. Dark Matter, or She Who Has No Name, needed help to fit the planets and the stars within her beautiful dress.

The Dominions help keep the order and the structure of time and dimensions. The Dominions are not often called upon for help since they are the framework, or the structure. The Dominions make up the foundation for the Web of Life that exists for each Universe. They work directly with She Who Has No Name to define areas and help with the process of creation. In restaurant, business and theatre terms, they are at the back of the house, working the back office or backstage.

The Dominions are the space holders. I have seen enormous grids that look like steel beams holding skyscrapers together. (In the following pages, one will come to understand how the steel that holds our tall buildings together is also a conscious being.) The Dominions control space wormholes, portals to the entire space-time continuum. One popular study of the Dominions is called Astrology.

Next, the Virtues were spawned to work with ע, or Compassion, to continue to do the work of Love from the Great Goddess. The Virtues would be represented in the arts as the Muses or the Goddesses of creativity, grace, beauty and all forms of Love. Originally, the Virtues designed planets and inspired various Star Being races. Later, they came to help humans in their spiritual life to stay the course and not be negatively affected by those who are not following *ALL*'s Will. Considered the Guardians of the Elementals, the Virtues are close to all planets, but especially fond of Terra.

The Virtues are also a very important part of the Material world – it is the beauty, the music, the feeling of ecstasy and the creation of all things. The Virtues would rule the Earth with perfectly sunlit rainbow days every day. I enjoy working with the Virtues. Their message of Love is consistent and through the heart.

The Powers are often thought of as being where the Web of Life is hosted or stored, but ultimately the Web of Life is not *held* by the Powers, it is *protected* by the Powers. The Powers are the busiest of all Beings of Light – even busier than Guardian Angels! These poor chaps have to constantly change the Web of Life – the path of each individual – because of Free Will. Like great web designers, every day in the Life Matrix the Powers keep the Godspark on track.

The Powers make up the third part of this grand Middle Love Choir. They fight against the Chaos which is created on Earth because of Free Will. In our daily lives, the Powers are always encouraging us to stay aligned with *ALL*'s Will, knowing that *ALL*'s Will is what we truly choose for ourselves in Love. The Powers inspire all sentient beings to stay the course and be part of the Web of Life, as each of our lives have an archetype to follow. When Chaos or Free Will is used against another being, the Powers make things right again.

The Powers are little personal assistants that work with every sentient being to keep it on their own personalized path, the path they chose in their pure God state before coming into the Earth Walk. On occasion people get caught up in the Chaos of other humans and there is no message or lesson in it for them. Sometimes things do 'just happen,' but the Powers always make sure things get back on track for the individual's steady march towards the End result, the full understanding of their Earth Walk.

Of all the Beings of Conscious Light, this Middle Love Choir can most easily be tracked or seen by humankind. What is called Astrology on Earth is a way of looking at the patterns that form a soul's life. One's birth information is quite literally written in the stars – what you, the individual soul, and *ALL* decided for this life's journey is already written in planets and the stars. Our Universe is the Book of Life, but because all sentient beings have Free Will, we don't always follow the pre-set course. It is the Powers and Virtues who reset the course to help one get back to one's personal plan, one's pre-birth celestial agreement.

The last section of the Orders, the Lower Love Choir are either Earth-bound or have direct contact with all beings here, Terrestrial and otherwise. This Third section, or Lower Love Choir of Conscious Beings of Light, were created when the Earth Walk formed and Terra became the learning planet that it is. The Lower Love Choir came into being because of a contract made on Terra. This is the moment when *ALL* created the last three Angelic orders to help all beings – Star Beings, Angelic Beings, everyone – in their conscious life on Terra. When one's soul achieves physical form on

Terra one receives a Being of Conscious Light (Guardian Angel) to help one find oneself. To find oneself is to find God, The Creator...to find *ALL*.

The Principalities, the Archangels and the Guardian Angels make up this Lower Love Choir. (Lower as in lower dimension. Remember that the sense of hierarchy is a human construction and not applicable to the Angelic realms). These are Beings of Conscious Light. One on Earth knows them best as Angels. These are the messengers of *ALL*, the carriers of Healing Love, of Conscious Light, of Unlimited Energy.

The Principalities set up the morals of the various Star Beings, helping these beings stay within certain spiritual beliefs and guiding the leaders towards *ALL*'s Will. The Principalities inspire Ascended Masters and guide us daily for the highest good of *ALL*.

The Principalities aid in the Heroic Journey to the self and support healings from the Archangels. They work hand in hand with the Powers to keep each Godspark steadfast on its own conscious path. Truly anything can happen at any minute because of Free Will. There is no judgment within the Angelic orders, no good or bad. It is simply that anything can happen and they are here to help us along our individual paths to Oneness.

The Archangels are not limited to church paintings and look nothing like the winged paintings. They are powerful beings of Pure Conscious Love Energy that can aid each and every one, but like all of the Beings of Light, one must call upon them for help. One's prayers stemming from Love are answered by Archangels.

This Lower Love Choir came to stop Chaos. Archangels were brought in as Warriors. They are trained elite soldiers of Compassion, a direct out-reaching of the Seraphim, expanding through all dimensions. Knowing that *ALL* could only be met in the presence of the Seraphim, the Archangels are ideal communicators for *ALL* with their unique vibration. They can directly report to *ALL* and they are also able to directly help the Terrestrials. These warriors make sure that Love and Compassion are always protected. They are also part of the Cherubim, so they do not allow anyone to destroy or harm the Akashic Records or to prematurely enter into *ALL*'s direct path before they are ready to complete their journey and be fully reabsorbed into *ALL*.

These great protectors have immense powers and abilities, however they are not allowed to directly kill any beings themselves. They can only help other beings defeat those that are using *ALL*'s work against *ALL* and going against God's Will. The archangels can heal, protect, strengthen, Love, inspire, and control nature to allow the highest good to flow for *ALL*'s Will and for *ALL*.

The final choir are the Guardian Angels. As with the Principalities and the Archangels, Guardian Angels came in with the Great Compact. Since then every being and Star Being in every Universe is born with at least one dedicated Guardian Angel. Whether one believes in angels or not doesn't matter. *ALL* created this angelic team so it would be guaranteed that every being would follow *ALL*'s Will. The Guardian Angels were created when Earth and humans were created in their present form. They are truly here to help with daily living.

Beings of Conscious Light Download Experience

Close your eyes and let your mind wander. Feel this history. See this history. Explore this history. Invite your Guardian Angel to lead you.

Notes

Notes

Free Will

When we speak of Free Will on Earth, people of Earth often cheer it on. Some people think Free Will means that we have a choice to do whatever we want in the present moment and can do whatever we feel like doing. That definition of Free Will is about choices and options such as capitalism versus abundance. That may be true, but there is far more to it, for that is not the full story.

The truth is, Free Will is the biggest obstacle on this planet. One pertinent example is the manner in which unrestrained capitalism - a result of misguided Free Will - goes against *ALL*'s Will.

Free Will, which was created to develop consciousness and encourage creativity and endless possibilities, has instead led to Chaos causing much confusion and anxiety. Free Will gives fear the opportunity to rule. *ALL*'s Will is defined as one's soul's purpose; what one sets out to do on this planet (Earth plane) before one is ever conceived or born. *ALL*'s Will is the soul star contract that is tied to one's star. It holds billions of years of light and knowledge with *ALL* and can be found in one's DNA.

Each individual gets to select what they want to do on this green learning planet before they come. We sit with Source - with *ALL* - and plan out our own lives in order to fully experience the thirteen archetypes. We look at what has been experienced and what is yet for us to experience. That is what is meant by Free Will, not human factors such as whether or not to drink alcohol at a given moment. One is FREE to choose one's path with one's Creator before one even arrives on this planet, and it is one's Free Will to choose whether to stick to this co-created plan or not.

Sticking to the plan brings one closer to Oneness and the return to *ALL*. Going off the plan extends the time that one travels on their journey of physical life. Will you remain for additional life cycles without learning the lessons you are here to learn? Again, there is no judgment. Only choice with Free Will.

This explains why Terrestrials have no memory of their past lives: It would defeat the purpose of experiencing Free Will. If one came in already knowing one's entire history, one wouldn't learn anything new, one might even go mad by recycling the past in an endless loop, getting caught in the karmic cycle like a gerbil doomed to run forever on a wheel of life to nowhere.

Understanding this, one now sees that there is no war of light and dark. One has been lied to by Chaos creating Chaos. There is no war. Instead, there is the parade, the pageant, of bringing everything back to the loving embrace of *ALL*'s Oneness. We are all on the journey to evolve back to the 1st dimension, yearning to be everything that *ALL* created in *ALL*'s Master Will or Master Web of Life, as there is only *ALL* in the end and in the beginning.

The Beings of Conscious Light can be seen as the soldiers and the worker bees of *ALL* and their purpose is clearly defined within *ALL's* Will. Light Beings have never, nor will they ever, turn against God Will, for they are directly part of *ALL*, just as we all are. The Beings of Conscious Light have no Free Will when in their perfect state. If and when a Being of Conscious Light wants to experience Free Will they go in physical form to Earth.

Free Will Download Experience

Close your eyes and let your mind wander. Feel this history. See this history. Explore your Will and ALL's Will for you.

Notes

Notes

Fallen Angels

The history and stories of Beings of Conscious Light falling from the Heavens into disgrace from *ALL*, such as the tale of the fallen Angel Lucifer, is not fully understood by most humans. There are no fallen Angels, only grounded Angels.

ALL does not judge. If a Being of Conscious Light chooses Free Will, it will then incarnate as a physical being on Earth with *ALL*'s Godspark for its Earth Walk. Most avatars or embodiments on Earth are Angels (Beings of Conscious Light), so most human beings carry an angelic soul. A few avatars have only Star Being lineage (more familiarly known on Earth as alien). Many hold both lineages, as Star Being lineage can be found in DNA.

Living as a human on Earth is to be a grounded Angel. This is the shared experience of the vast majority of humans. We are nearly all grounded Angels. Star Being lineage often becomes misunderstood as well. They, too, are on their Earth Walk, learning and growing. All are on a journey to return to *ALL*. We are One at heart. We are One in Love.

Fallen Angels Download Experience

Close your eyes and let your mind wander. Feel this history. See this history. Explore this history.

Notes

Notes

Physical Creation

The first physical beings were not of the Angelic order. The first physical beings created by *ALL* were microscopic and are now called protons and neutrons. They had no mouths. They had no eyes. They were pure vibration, the pure physical energy vibration of Love. They were part of a duplicating process that was neither masculine nor feminine, but were simply *ALL*. These beings could be described as hermaphrodite as they each carried both masculine and feminine qualities. These beings were able to produce a duplicate of themselves and elevate in an instant. The Beings of Conscious Light were there to help create the spiritual link and space for them to elevate.

What started out as twelve Seed Beings, or the Egg of Life, multiplied faster and faster. Soon these tiny beings created so many billions of themselves that they began to form the physical. These twelve Seed Beings were *ALL*'s Children of Light. They were many things: sound, Spirit, Love from the founders – the Original Creator beings. The Seed Beings formed the twelve archetypes, with *ALL* as the thirteenth Archetype. *ALL* is the First Original Creator Being in the Tree of Life.

This is also when the Elementals were created, when we get our first Beings that were not just of Light but also of the physical body. This is when Ba of the Original Creator Circles formed physical life. Like a mad scientist, Ba was exploding with creation. The protons and neutrons formed the elements – the building blocks of life – through Sacred Geometry. As the Elementals exploded outward, it instantly created planets in billions of galaxies, among them a planet called Terra.

As *ALL* continued to expand and grow, so did all other Beings. It is said that the Anunnaki were the first full physical Beings created directly by Ba.

After the Anunnaki, other organisms were created for other planets and in other dimensions. The next Beings to have life were the Draconian, the Mantis, the Sirius, the Hathor's, the Pleiadeans and, later, the Arcturians, Martians, and Valerians. Hundreds of different species of life were created across galaxies. So many different Beings, each in their own area, growing and expanding so that each of them may become One with *ALL* again.

Some of these Beings have met each other, while some have nothing to do with the others. Some Beings appear as very boring creatures in the minds of humans – they are seen by us as building blocks, as parts, not as full Beings on their own account. Some of these different life forces no longer exist; they played small but important roles for *ALL*'s purposes and their work is done. They have each played their part in one way or another, for they were created by *ALL*.

One of the original Creator beings, ע Compassion/*Love,* is part of the source of *ALL*. *Love* went to work, inspiring the Beings of Conscious Light – making them burn out of Compassion for *ALL*. This burning is often mistaken for passion which creates war and death. It is energy. *Love* is unlimited eternal unconditional energy for *ALL*'s *everything*.

ע Compassion/*Yin/Love* also had some of its greatest influence over several other entities, including the Blue Arcturians, the Pleiadians, Sirius (Dog Star people) and eventually the White Zeta. These and several other beings, including the Hathors, embraced Compassion and lived their lives according to *ALL*'s Compassion and the Will (or purpose) that was defined for each of their individual Godsparks. Harmony and peace continues to ring through their lives as individuals.

The whole of the Universe can now be seen far, far past *ALL*'s first thought. She Who Has No Name has expanded so quickly, yet she holds the dimensions carefully and with the greatest precision ever, each layer with its own unique dimensions.

Some layers exist of only sound or light vibration. These layers are the oldest dimensions as they were the first cry of life. Om is still heard. The vibrations they give off of sound and color are the closest dimension to the first conscious thought. They *are* Om.

So much creation was happening at once. Planets of many different kinds; some that burn with fire and gases and some that are so very green with water and strange plants; Each one creating its own structure of life, according to *ALL*. *ALL* has a plan and purpose for every one of its creations. Including one.

Understanding that Creation happened instantly without time or definition allowed Consciousness & Compassion to flourish throughout the Void. ע Compassion (*Love*) & Consciousness (OM) put themselves into physical form with the help of Ba. Ba wanted to experience the joining of these two Original Creator Beings. One successful collaboration was planet Terra. Having a planet that was an absolute balance of the two Original Creator Beings would be a step closer to Oneness.

Terra was born by Ba during the creation of the Elementals. She was kept in a private space in the back of She Who Has No Name's skirt.

Terra was a blue-green planet that wasn't quite as explosive as other planets; not hot like stars, but not quite as chilled as an asteroid. As such, Terra was allowed to evolve and grow on her own. She was a small planet compared to all other planets, but her soul was directly from ע Compassion (*Love*) & Consciousness (OM). Her core would be Crystalline Love, burning, beating; the hot heart of Love burning from within. Terra would be covered in secrecy being held at the very edge, upon the middle layer of She with No Name's skirt.

The story of Terra is this: She was created by Ba when the Elementals were created. She was allowed to expand, evolve and grow on her own with all the Elementals. Just like every other planet, all the same opportunities and information was given out, but it was up to Terra to grow with the information. She was special. With the help of Ka, Terra expanded the Godspark inside her core, for she is part of *ALL*. The Godspark inside of Terra was directly from Compassion (*Love*) & Consciousness (OM). Since she was both Compassion (*Love*) & Consciousness (OM), Terra expanded out faster, creating new life within her small area, spinning and dancing all over the Milky Way. Terra's beginnings are the true Love story of life, that of the Divine Masculine and Divine Feminine blended together as Conscious Love.

Terra was a volatile planet. She hadn't gotten the moon or the sun to settle in with her yet. They were not warring, they just hadn't developed a good relationship yet. Terra was young with no rules. She was like a child, exploring and feeling what she was. She would play in the wrong areas and get pummeled by asteroids. Spinning without fear, she continued expanding.

The Moon was continually revolving at an unregulated speed. This caused different effects upon Terra from monsoons to surges of huge tsunamis, even earthquakes splitting her apart at places. The Sun, Ra, the closest star would flare up and singe Terra's lands, for she only had the simple protective cover of the clouds. Her backside would freeze while her front broiled in Ra's light. It was a chaotic time, but an amazing time for the growth of new life using the powerful building blocks created by *ALL*.

For billions of cycles Terra was left alone to create herself. She built up mountains, dried up oceans, froze her lands and then de-[illegible] them rapidly. She founded small life forms that could handle her changing moods as she spun first one direction and then the other, dancing around Ra. Terra fell in love with Ra and hung around him, fully knowing his passion for her could burn her to infinity.

Slowly the Sun and Moon embraced a perfect harmony, feeling out the exact distance that worked best for Terra and themselves. Close enough for Terra to feel Ra's love warming her, but not so close that his Compassion hurt her crust. She hummed with life in this small space on the edge of the middle dimension of the Void.

In human terms this took place over billions of years, but for *ALL* it was the space of one breath. Time and space does not exist for *ALL* like it does for us on planet Earth. What we measure as huge amounts of time becomes nothing but a sigh when *ALL* and the Original Creator beings look at it.

Terra, this beautiful green watery planet, buzzed with its own abundant life, but this was not seen by the other Beings that had been created by *ALL* in the Multiverse. Terra went unnoticed for an immeasurable amount of time, for every one of the other Beings *ALL* had created first had to find themselves. They had to live out the purpose *ALL* had given them. It was only once they had reached a proper level of growth that the opportunity came to reach outside of their realms and explore what they understood as life in other places.

Physical Creation Download Experience

Close your eyes and let your mind wander. Feel this history. See this history. Explore this history.

Notes

ALL's Power Desired

As everything in creation continued to expand, so did a desire to be *ALL* or to posess *ALL's* power. This created a need for additional Protectors beyond those protecting the Akashic Records. Special Protectors were needed to be Protectors of *ALL*'s Will. *ALL* then created the choir of Beings of Conscious Light called the Archangels. These Archangels were created to be great Protectors, helping to address the chaos and fighting that had already begun.

ALL saw how his entities had begun to turn against each other. Several lineages of Star Beings felt that one lineage should rule over the others. This was not in the original plan, yet it was foreseen and fully expected.

ALL thought that each of the entities existed in their own space, and that many of them did not need to expand out, but some of the entities had been given access to so much knowledge, so much freedom that, as we would say in human terms, their egos took over and they wanted everything. These entities developed a god-like complex and felt that they were gods. They believed that they held the same level of power as the Original Creator Beings.

These entities began a separation from *ALL*. Having lost their connection to *ALL*, they could no longer understand fully what their purpose was, becoming even more disconnected. They started to make their own creatures so these subservient creatures could revere the entities as gods.

Various Star Beings began to violently take over planets and regions, even destroying some societies completely. This is the source of the many stories and myths of great Angelic wars and the alleged fall of the Light Beings.

These tales are not true. The Light Beings have always worked only for the True Source. They have worked only for *ALL*. It is the Star Beings whose souls come from the stars and suns that turned against *ALL*. Any fables you have heard of fallen Angels are actually true tales of Star Beings going against *ALL*'s Will.

ALL's Power Desired Download Experience

Close your eyes and let your mind wander. Feel this history. See this history. Explore this history.

Notes

The Anunnaki

The Anunnaki were one of the Star Beings that went against *ALL*'s Will. The Anunnaki were made to be creators. As with several other Star Beings, the Anunnaki had their own technology, their own new knowledge that they were expanding upon.

What is known on Earth as Genetics was one of the Anunnaki's greatest areas of accomplishment. The problem was not that the Anunnaki were creating new beings; the problem was that the Anunnaki were teaching these new beings that the Anunnaki was the one true creator, leaving out all mention of *ALL*. The Anunnaki felt that science ruled the Universe and *ALL* did not matter anymore.

One of the first beings they created is what we on Earth know as Zeta Reticulan Greys. The Zeta were created by the Anunnaki. At first the act of creation was for the benefit of higher science and higher knowledge. Some Zeta became slaves to perform domestic duties, others were built to be warriors. This was the first form of Artificial Intelligence, but it took place in a live being, not a mechanical one. The development of the Zetas took many trials. Thousands of different life forms were failures, but soon the Anunnaki were able to create these beings and they created massive amounts of them.

Over much time the Zetas evolved from being slaves and warriors to members of their own society. They created their own organizational structure, having their own rules and regulations. Soon the Zetas' intelligence began to expand as they figured out how to replicate themselves, creating more and more of their kind, expanding outward with other Star Beings and creating new hybrids. It would be considered today that they built the first robots and they gained their own consciousness. (At some point, one will understand the robot is a conscious being because it is made up from elementals.)

Like the stories throughout time of so many different enslaved beings, after many years the Zeta gained their own thoughts. By finding their own conscious connection to Ka, the Spirit of the Godspark, and the other Original Creator Beings, a large group of the Zeta were able to break away from the Anunnaki. They connected large groups of spaceships to create a new world where they could thrive.

In this new environment they moved away from the neutral quality to more of a masculine quality and they began to create hybrids. They cloned themselves with other beings, making hybrids, including the White Zetas. Later in their development they used human DNA to create inspirational toys to teach their children about Compassion. What started out as artificial intelligence, as a simple robot, over time became a conscious living being that created its own peaceful society.

At first this new technology, this new power, did not help to ease the wars. Instead it just created more confusion and distrust. As though life had no meaning, the Zetas and their other new beings destroyed as much as they created. A few mistakes were made and some got punished. There are unlimited amounts of events, stories and myths that came from this, so many perspectives, so many beings.

The Anunnaki Download Experience

Close your eyes and let your mind wander. Feel this history. See this history. Explore this history.

Notes

Notes

Nin-Khursag

One story that does affect one greatly is the story of an Anunnaki Princess who was very much into Genetics and the creation of new life.

Nin-Khursag saw how the Zetas had gone off into their own destiny with great success. She was very proud that they were partly of her design, with her father and mother completing the actual process. Nin-Khursag was up for a new challenge. All in the name of science to find the perfect being, she performed some risqué experiments and was banned from the University or Central Learning District.

One of her closest companions was on an exploratory mission not to conquer, but to find new ally planets. He was sent out into all time, all dimensions and all space to find new entities and introduce himself to them, or possibly seize them on behalf of the Annunaki. They also watched other Star Beings who might invade them. Kind of like Star Trek, they were explorers in space. It was this explorer who accidentally found the Planet Terra on his way to Mars. He thought this little untouched planet would be a perfect petri dish for Nin-Khursag and her experiments.

Once the information of this planet got to her, she quickly insisted that the explorer take her to this new planet. Nin-Khursag was particularly intrigued by this place since it had life that had grown organically, untouched by superior beings. It was as though *ALL* had one planet out of a billion planets that was able to expand freely out of a balance of Compassion and consciousness. This little blue-green planet was full of Love and unlimited possibilities.

As the two Anunnaki travelers began to explore their newfound treasure, they realized it needed a little help to truly expand

and become the ultimate place for testing. Its location was ideal since it was already hidden so there would be few controls to limit their experimentation. Nin-Khursag worked with Star Beings from realms other than her own to set the Moon in place so it no longer created huge tsunamis on Terra.

With Star Being technology, the Princess was able to create a stronger gravitational pull on the planet to hold everything down and give it more physical form. The average planet doesn't have gravity, or not quite as much gravity as we now experience on Earth. They are much more fluid. Here on this giant rock known as Terra, they needed to create more options and lighten up the heaviness of the planet to make it a perfect setting for the new life she and other experimenters would create.

As the Sirius or Dogstar People were some of the first Star Beings on this planet, they had already made first contact with the indigenous people of the planet. Through its own evolution, *ALL* had already created several types of "trunk beings" on Terra. Trunk beings are those beings which have arms and legs coming out of a Center Point. Most of these beings had evolved from the slugs, mitochondria and plasma of the beginning of time. The Sirius came and gave them more potential to flourish as a race. Being very careful in how they approached the new life, the Sirians always stayed within *ALL*'s requests.

More Star Beings came to this planet as a place to experiment. The first beings that Nin-Khursag created were the centaurs, as she crossed the trunk being with a horse. She tried several forms. She crossed the trunk beings with goats, and with fish. She also worked on perfecting the size of the human form, from miniature to giant. Many forms, sizes and shapes were experimented with and created over an extended period of time.

Nin-Khursag would create small communities and study them until they all died. Some of her beings would live 400 years, and some survived only 4 days. There are some of her creations still swimming in the deeper depths of the ocean, free from her captivity and never to be found. None of them achieved her goal of creating the perfect physical form.

The Anunnaki Princess pondered on and on, ultimately deciding to start with an original being from this compassionate planet and put in her Consciousness, her knowledge. She thought that by blending in her DNA, she could create the ultimate being. She even found an indigenous person worthy to mate with. None of the beings resulting from this union lived very long, if they even made it through birth.

Other entities, the Hathors, the Sirians, had come from other planets to create. They, too, began to play with the creatures of this planet. Some of these space travelers only wanted to inspire Terra, helping her grow as *ALL*'s Will lead. Others, entities from far distant places, wanted to conquer and enslave Terra. A few of the Star Beings came to collect some of Terra's indigenous creatures, enslaving them taking them far away, never to return.

Much time passed while this planet served as a testing ground for many Star Beings. These Star Beings built enormous structures that imprisoned their test subjects. Huge cities built up over night, like giant Universities, all connecting into one round center structure. The original purpose of one notable structure, Atland, was not to be a thriving city, but to be a large scale laboratory. Later Atland would become the foundation for Atlantis.

Nin-Khursag Download Experience

Close your eyes and let your mind wander. Feel this history. See this history. Explore this history.

Notes

Atland

Atland was seen as a compound for a universal scientific genetic study. It was like a university city, where Star Beings could purchase labor or custom design an Artificial Intelligence to be harvested as a food source, or experiment on new beings by adding their own DNA. The entire city was covered in high technology that appeared like a shield of gold dust to blur the view of *ALL*'s Conscious Beings of Light and keep the planet hidden from any who would object to the experiments and industry that was taking place on Terra. The trading of humans, humanoids, and other Star Beings were happening under the radar. Well run factories and high technology farms were raising beings for consumption, experimentation and labor.

Part of Atland brought new magic to Terra, opening small vortexes of realms linking to distant planets. Dimensional Portals were built like giant underground train stations, allowing Star Beings from the multiverse to come and go with ease. No spaceships clouded the skies.

On a distant planet in another galaxy during one of the key battles of the Archangels, strange trunk being slaves were discovered. The Archangels were not familiar with this form or this new technology that had come from Terra. Once these Angelic Beings of Conscious Light were made aware of what was happening on and to Terra, they immediately went to her aid.

Terra, smaller than most planets, was such an unknown planet it truly had gone unnoticed, but since Terra was Compassion embodied, she was very special to the Original Creator Beings. For a very long time the Light Beings had been tricked by the gold dust clouds that covered the massive experimental city. Eventually nearly every Star Being race was found to be hiding experiments and large communities in Atland.

Following the discovery of the odd trunk being slaves the Light Beings came to Terra and began to question what was happening. Here was this innocent, naïve, Love planet that was supposed to be allowed to evolve on its own in its own purity. It was to be untouched by anything, with only Love and Compassion allowing it to expand in *ALL*'s Will. Unfortunately, it had been found and it had felt the effects of the outsiders. From the experiments, many new beings were now on this planet, beings that did not come from *ALL*'s directive. *ALL*'s original plan for Terra had been destroyed.

Atland Download Experience

Close your eyes and let your mind wander. Feel this history. See this history. Explore this history.

Notes

The Great War of Wars

ALL's original Star Being creations had found a way to sidestep and move out of *ALL*'s will. On Terra they could have Free Will. Through these rogue Star Beings a new atmosphere and controls had been put on Terra, sending her to the lower dimensions, to the deepest part of the galaxy to hide. These beings did not follow with *ALL*'s Will or with what *ALL* had planned for this young planet to be.

This was unacceptable.

The Beings of Light came to Terra's aid, but the Star Beings did not give up their power easily. Huge battles raged across the planet and in her atmosphere. The Great War of Wars took place. It may even be called the Lucifer Fall. Terra, once the planet of Compassion and Love, was faced with total destruction.

There are a number of sites on this planet where one can still see the destruction from this battle, huge cuts into Terra that are now deep in her oceans. Legends across the multiverse have been written about this millennial battle for control. As above so below – here were all the problems of the multiverse now being held in one space, on one small planet.

Archangel Gabriel blew his horn to end the great wars on Terra. The Conscious Beings of Light had uncovered the truth and destroyed the gold dust shield. They had battled and won. But now it was time to decide Terra's future. This is when all of the Star Beings – not just the rogue experimenters – became conscious of Terra, learning of the reckless activity and atrocities of some of their fellow Star Beings. As awareness of the Great War of Wars and of the experimentations that had gone against *ALL*'s Will grew across the multiverse, the Star Beings were faced with a choice: All

Star Beings and Terra either must be terminated and come to an end or they must all commit to an agreement in order for Terra's life to be saved.

Ultimately, the various Star Beings from all over the multiverse came to peace. A great Intergalactic Council was created to represent all the various Star Beings, giving all beings in the Universe representation as plans were made to either correct or incorporate the damage done and move forward under *ALL*.

The Great War of Wars Download Experience

Close your eyes and let your mind wander. Feel this history. See this history. Explore this history.

<u>Notes</u>

The Intergalactic Council

The first order of business for the Intergalactic Council was dealing with the aftermath of The Great War of Wars on Terra, cleaning up Terra and putting her back together after major sections of her had been destroyed. Then they had to deal with Atland and understand what the Anunnaki Princess had been doing on this planet, for it was she who had founded Atland. Other Star Beings in Atland were also charged with going against *ALL*'s Will on the hidden planet.

A great debate began as they began to rebuild Terra.

The Intergalactic Council had to work with the Beings of Conscious Light trying to put together a contract to decide what to do with this Green Planet. It had already been tampered with, yet it was in the newly defined neutral zone, so it needed to be left alone. Some members of the Intergalactic Council truly believed it was best to leave the planet alone to undo what had been done. The Pure Conscious Beings, like what one would call Vulcan, really wanted to walk away and let Terra be. They wanted everything to be undone, for *ALL* could easily fix anything or do anything.

The debate continued on for time unknown as the planet, herself, continued to grow. The influences of the Great War of Wars and its conclusion were already changing the planet's outcome. Eventually a decision was made and a unique plan was outlined by Archangel Mikkel.

It was decided that at this point it was too late to turn back. Star alliances had already been made in several different ways with different Beings. As the Intergalactic Council sat in their great discussions, the suggestion was brought forward that this planet should be used for its original purpose – **for *ALL***. Terra should be a place to truly experience Love and Compassion in an area that allowed Free Will. If Beings were given choices – if they were given Free Will – in a space that was designed for Love and Compassion it would help *ALL* manifest itself back to Oneness quicker.

The Intergalactic Council Download Experience

Close your eyes and let your mind wander. Feel this history. See this history. Explore this history.

Notes

The Plan of Archangel Mikkel

Archangel Mikkel, the first Seraphim created in form, came to the conclusion that Terra could be the learning planet for *ALL* beings, be they the Light Beings or the Star Beings created by *ALL*. The first step, Mikkel suggested, was that the Godspark be placed into the trunk beings that had been created, as well as into every other being created on Terra. They would all be given the Godspark through a Sun Soul.

The second step was to give both Light Beings and Star Beings the opportunity to join with a trunk being in a unique blending of spirit and body in order to feel life on Terra. Furthermore, each Sun Soul on Terra would be directly tied to *ALL*, as well as to every Soul in the Universe.

Not only did Archangel Michael suggest that *ALL* give the trunk beings a direct spark of life, but Archangel Michael also proposed that this small learning Planet be a place where all Beings could experience Free Will. With Free Will on a Love planet, every Star Being could learn how to get along with one another and how to tolerate and accept each other, instead of having wars and battles, for by now all Universes and planes and dimensions had grown to know bitter conflict.

The concept was to stop the fighting and incessant killing that was taking place on and between their planets by giving all Star Beings the opportunity to learn Compassion and Consciousness on Terra. They would put every type of Star Being into one place allowing total learning to happen. "As Above, So Below," Mikkel said.

The council stood in awe of this concept. That through *ALL*, they could put themselves on this planet of trunk beings and learn how to get along – this was unheard of!

Free Will. The concept seemed impossible, but desired. The Galactic Council thought it unimaginable to have Free Will. All past models and experiments using Free Will inevitably led to ultimate self-destruction. Only *ALL*'s active presence could overcome this inevitability, bringing an outcome of peace and understanding through Compassion and Consciousness. All other attempts without *ALL* had failed...yet look how long Atland existed before they got caught by the Seraphim. Perhaps destruction wasn't as inevitable as previously thought.

Mikkel began to get the different entities to agree upon this great plan. Once the Council members all agreed, the plan would be presented to *ALL*. Terra could become the one place where everyone would exist within the same physical format. Everyone would share the same opportunities in the same physical form, but without the advantages of eternal life or of all knowledge. It was a worthy experiment, an ambitious plan. They called it The Great Compact.

The Plan of Archangel Mikkel Download Experience

Close your eyes and let your mind wander. Feel this history. See this history. Explore this history and what it means to you.

Notes

The Great Compact

The Great Compact was presented to *ALL* with the blessing of the Great Intergalactic Council.

ALL considered this ambitious plan which had been originated by Archangel Mikkel and saw many advantages. By enacting so much life experience on just one tiny planet, the rest of the Universe could continue to expand out the way it was originally meant to. *ALL* fully knew that the experience of everything was the purpose of existence, as that had always been *ALL*'s plan. Now this vast array of experience could take place on Terra.

ALL agreed to give Ka, the Consciousness Spirit, to the trunk beings and other entities of Terra as long as every Star Being and Light Being agreed that they, too, would donate a part of their soul so that they could experience life on Terra, which was now coming to be known as the planet Earth. The Star Beings and Light Beings would have a place to learn, to understand, and to grow together so that they could come back to Oneness again in *ALL*. *ALL* reminded all of the Beings that they were all made up of *ALL* and that every molecule within them was the spark of life from the Source from the Beginning of Time.

It was through the Compassion that was the heart of *ALL* that everyone and everything would learn to get along, and as this harmony was achieved, one by one, each and every Being joining the experience would return to the Oneness of *ALL*.

To accomplish this, every aspect in the Universe was shrunk down to one plane, to this one location, to allow Free Will – the ability to pre-choose the path of each journey on Earth in order for each Star Being and Light Being to experience the wide variety of

·rything over a series of lifetimes – to bring peace to *ALL*'s many and varied creations.

ALL agreed to Mikkel's plan for this one planet to allow Free Will. This way every entity, every being on the test planet could experience existence for *ALL*. The Great Compact would allow a specific amount of time for the Star Beings to aid their new blended creations, but the Beings of Conscious Light would be used as the consistent form for the Soul. This would give Angels a chance to be physical and experience Free Will, as well.

ALL decided to give the individual Sun Souls & Planet Souls on Earth Free Will unlike anywhere else. Before the Sun Souls and the Planet Souls of the Star Beings entered this planet, each would make an agreement on who they wanted to be, what lessons they wanted to learn, and how they wanted to learn it. Each soul manifested itself with *ALL* exactly the way they wanted to be. Elsewhere, all other beings created with a Godspark have *ALL*'s purpose with *ALL*'s intentions and *ALL*'s intentions are always to come back to Oneness, to the Source of *ALL*.

With this new freedom Earth truly could be a learning planet. In this grand experiment, *ALL* decided that every type of being would live on this planet. The Anunnaki could find out if their knowledge, their DNA, is truly that of the greatest leaders, as they think they are. They would learn if they truly do have infinite knowledge in comparison with others, because each Annunaki soul would be embedded into the same physical form as a Mantis, as a Hathor, as a Draconian. Every being would be in equal form, with an equal opportunity to grow and learn.

This created a great opportunity for *ALL* to allow the chaos of Free Will, but in a confined place.

The Great Compact Download Experience

Close your eyes and let your mind wander. Feel this history. See this history. Explore this history.

Notes

Notes

The Great Compact Begins

The Great Compact created the greatest experiment ever. Earth as the learning planet! What an exciting time it was. As one book says, humans were created in the likeness of God, however, there is no likeness of God, for God is God. There is no likeness of *ALL*, for *ALL* is *ALL*. It was the likeness created by the Anunnaki that won out for overall structure and functionality.

Since Princess Nin-Khursag had created the most reliable form for this planet in the various trunk people forms that existed, her design was chosen to be the final form. Her lasting signature or "Mark of the Avatar" is called the Eve Gene and it is found in every human's DNA. She was the designer of the human body.

The human race was created based on the Anunnaki design with a trunk body standing upright on two feet, with two arms. There were at least 10 different trunk being societies on this planet before The Great Compact. With The Great Compact, these all had to be removed so that one specific form could create a standard foundation.

Only a few modifications were made to this form from the Great Intergalactic Council recommendations. With these few minor adjustments, everyone could feel involved in the final creation. Each entity from the Hathor's to the Mantis added something different to the DNA, each giving specific human qualities or human ethnicities. They were the gods, giving each basic trunk being the DNA of these specific qualities, then adding their own specific Star Being DNA to the mixture. The Star Beings were allowed to help or rule their group of Terrestrials for a set number of years, as it was written in the stars.

The Anunnaki, already having roots at Atland, took this as their starting place for this new era. Each race of Star Beings was able to create the same ratio of beings on this planet as exist in their worlds. For example, the Hathor's DNA, being very musically inclined, is known to have founded the Egyptians and Tibetans. There were the Mantis, the Felines, the Draconians, Zetas and other Star Beings, each selecting different regions and populating them with their specific DNA in their blood. The DNA is carried out by showing physical likeness as well as certain spiritual or moral beliefs. Other Star Beings also influenced Egyptians, like the Sekhmet, Feline race, as well as the Andromedan race. The Anabua race has its physical qualities in many indigenous races, including Polynesian and Mongolian.

ALL approved the plan that all Star Beings may have an option to go live on the learning planet. However, all of the guiding or ruling Star Beings and deities had to leave the planet after the agreed upon time in order to see how the Terrestrials would thrive on their own.

The Star Beings were allotted thousands of years to create an infrastructure and their own unique paradigms or belief structures before leaving. If the Star Beings wanted to return to Terra after that, they had to come in human form through the Godspark. Until such time as every Soul became balanced with Consciousness and Compassion, returning to *ALL*, the Star Beings were to let Terra expand, untouched, with her new purpose.

As soon as *ALL* approved The Great Compact, Ka went to work within an instant. With the Godspark, Beings were activated with a new soul consciousness. Terra already had life, but now these lifeforms had a Godspark that not only included Compassion, but also had representation from all of the Universe's different interdimensional species and entities. Even species that had no physical existence received physical form as humans or other entities on this learning planet.

The entirety of this creation would exist on one plane – the 3rd dimension – on this one planet. As an example, the beings that live in the dimensions of only vibration or sound (where OM lives) needed to participate in this planet as well.

The dimensions where only vibration exists were able to co-exist in the same dimensional layout of a physically heavier, lower vibrational planet like Terra in a unique way. They did not become homo sapiens. Instead, they manifested their Soul or Godspark inside the gemstones and rocks that were already in existence on this mother planet. Here, they could increase their vibration and their knowledge, bringing new wisdom to the planet, while also taking back additional knowledge to their own dimensions.

The planet Earth was designed to stay within the median range, or the average of all opportunities. It would be considered Middle Earth, a place where all different dimensions and time in space exist. Earth was selected to sit right in the middle of all parallel Universes.

The decision was made that all creations not indigenous to Terra would be wiped out or destroyed to create a clean slate so the naturally evolved animals and the newly created homo sapiens on the planet would all be at the same starting position. A few of the experimental creatures, such as mermaids, sasquatch, and other beings, either hid or were overlooked during this initial cleansing of the planet.

If one thinks about it, The Great Compact created a situation that was really quite ideal when one sees how truly vast the Universe is. The Universe is so incredibly expansive, one can never tell where it ends or begins. This lone planet, Terra, was selected because it was so perfect with its naturally evolving life forms, even after all the years of rogue Star Being interference.

Terra was just a small droplet in the gigantic Universe. When Terra was first discovered, she existed in the Second Dimension.

She had a life force all her own. Terra's obscure size meant that the activities of the Great Compact would not affect the greater Universe or any of the vibrational dimensions and planes. Terra went from being a problem, a hidden place of out of control experimentation and disregard for *ALL*'s Will, to becoming the perfect location for this grand experiment within the heart of *ALL*.

This was a time described in the Mayan calendar as an origin story. The initiation of The Great Compact (also known as the Great Experiment) required that Terra's life force be increased. *ALL* sped up Terra's life force from the second dimension into the third dimension so that life could flourish in new ways. This is where the great experiment took Terra to the next level.

Terra, herself, agreed to be a part of the Great Experiment and became Middle Earth. The creatures that already inhabited her became more than just space creatures; Now they had Star Souls with a direct link to *ALL*. Terra's moon was even graced with the Goddess of Compassion. One knows of the Man in the Moon, but truly it is woman, the Goddess of Compassion, living there to keep a close eye on her earthly creation and to maintain the perfect rhythm for Terra.

Because this planet was so tiny in comparison to other planets, beings that were huge in their native lands would become small as miniscule beings became large, the better to experience contrast. The Mantis people would go from 15 to 20 feet in height down to two inches. The strongest would become the weakest and the weakest would become the strongest. Some of the races, including the reptilian race, who were a part of The Great Compact were considered the weakest. Now they would have an opportunity on this planet to become the strongest, all in the interest of experience and learning.

This Great Experiment on this learning Planet would not only allow the greatest to become the weakest and the weakest to become the strongest, but it put every Dimension, every plane, every entity onto one planet. In the depths of the ocean, hidden in the forest, in the life of the jungle and in the desert, all of the different entities throughout all of the Universe, throughout all of the planets, were able to find an environment on this planet where they could exist.

The Great Compact Begins Download Experience

Close your eyes and let your mind wander. Feel this history. See this history. Explore The Great Compact.

Notes

Notes

The Experiment Takes Place

For this Great Compact to truly be successful, a way was needed to store the experiences from all the various souls. The Seraphim worked with the Cherubim to create a whole new branch of the Akashic Records. All the highest level Dragons expanded to hold this new division.

In human terms, one would see the Akashic Records as an enormous digital cloud library of every single being in *ALL*'s Universes. The Akashic Records are *ALL*'s library of *ALL* knowledge. It holds the records of every sentient being, not only from Earth, but from the history of *ALL*, so for every Star Being as well. I, The Dragon Heart, dance with She Who Has No Name, holding the space of these records for *ALL*.

These records keep track. Once *ALL* has experienced everything the process of creation shall go into reverse and bring everything back to the one Source, back to *ALL*.

Every being on Terra was given eternal life through the Godspark. Their souls having the Godspark from *ALL*, they had access to incredible knowledge and unending wisdom. At the Godspark level, every being on Terra knew the history of creation. From the explosion of the Big Bang meeting of *ALL* and She Who Has No Name, instantly we have gone through the fabric of space with the sound of the first Om.

From the first entities, the Seraphim, to the creation of a physical body with the Anunnaki and other Star Beings, to this moment where *ALL* allowed the unthinkable to be done and gave consciousness to everything on planet Terra. The direct piece of Godspark from the Great Source of *ALL* and the soul donations from the Star Beings would ultimately shape the human race, but it was the *ALL* Conscious Light and She Who Has No Name who allowed for the creation of these systems to make it all happen.

It did happen and it was magnificent.

Instantly, everything happened and new conscious life sprang up all over the planet. Everything on Terra from rocks to plants to trees to the animals was given a Godspark spirit. Trees were embedded with knowledge as well as becoming the antennas for the Akashic Records. The trees, also known as "the standing people," were placed on the planet so information could be sent up. The trees are also here to absorb the pain of the planet, herself. One can tell if a tree is absorbing pain – it has burls on it. Trees are sacred, as they take on as much pain as they can from Mother Terra.

Water is the telecommunication or Wi-Fi of the world. It is through water that information from the ocean to the arctic ice caps is sent back and forth. Nature communicates with all of her plants and animals through Water. Nature tells them when the seasons will change, when food will be abundant and when the fires will come. Water is the closest element to *ALL* or Source outside of one's Godspark and the power of many rituals go to and through water.

The Plant and Animal People would nourish the bodies of the trunk beings. The Sky People would protect the new beings from the high and low vibrations from other galaxies and stars. The Stone People would record the history of Terra and help with her future formation. The systems on planet Terra were upgraded so they could fully support all the different life forms of all of the different entities from all over the Universe. Even the moon was adjusted to sit in the perfect location to keep the new rhythm of the planet consistent.

In the beginning of Middle Earth and its new form as the learning planet, new life sprung up everywhere. At first the Star Beings were very much interested in how the beings of Earth would grow or how they needed to be ruled. The Star Beings would come to Earth in the form of deities and gods. They not only inspired the systems of life on Earth, they also began to channel in new sources of information with passion. This was in the ancient history of Atlantis and the times when Lemuria flourished.

As time passed and the life form entities on planet Earth began to grow and expand, they began to take on the same problems as existed above in other realms. As Above, So Below. Soon wars began to take over Earth again; Wars for control over food, water, land and technology. At various times in history the Star Beings would come down onto the planet and try to change this violent situation. Again and again they tried to help the human race expand out to discover and enact new solutions of peace and sharing, but the humans never learned their lessons. The corruption and corrosion allowed through Free Will (the choice not to follow one's pre-birth plan for growth and expansion in physical life) lead to more wars and the extinction of races.

As the Spirits inside the life forms grew with each physical life experience, new knowledge would come to each human, opening doors for the creation of new information. Every time a soul entered back into a physical body on Earth their memories were wiped clean so that all lessons could be truly learned. There were records capturing everything in the Akashic Records, but the Soul encapsulated in the human form needed to experience everything clean and new each time. That is why Earth is considered a learning or teaching planet, because every time one's soul steps foot on this planet all memory of one's past life – or lives – is wiped out. All is meant to be forgotten so learning can happen from all angles and all possibilities.

It is up to each individual soul to discover who he or she truly is and what the purpose is for their current lifetime on this planet.

ALL spiraled out of each atom into the planet to experience everything. *ALL* allowed the Light Beings to protect the Godspark, to protect every Soul Being. *ALL* is a part of everything on the planet – with *ALL*'s strongest and most direct connection to the human beings.

ALL has never been separate from this planet or from any sentient being. *ALL*'s actions are felt through the Light Beings.

During the time of the Great Compact, before the Great Experiment began, *ALL* created the last Order of Angels – the Guardian Angels. *ALL* decided it was very important to give help to each being on Earth posessing a heart-beat and decreed that every animal, every human, every creature, shall be given a Guardian Angel to help it throughout its life. Even Terra received her own Guardian Angel, Sophia, to protect her inner core.

Success must be achievable. *ALL* ruled that each human being be given everything needed to complete its purpose successfully. These sentient beings are given all the help they desire, provided they ask for the help. Sentient beings must be able to receive Love and Consciousness in order to grow, in order to progress to their next stage. The Great Experiment continued.

The Experiment Takes Place Download Experience

Close your eyes and let your mind wander. Feel this history. See this history. Explore this space.

Notes

Notes

These messages are for the world.
These messages are for *you*.
These messages are for *now*

Opportunities

It was during the Great Compact that the archetypes were established, Thirteen types from the Fruit of Life. Each soul had to completely understand each of the thirteen archetypes in order to pass back into *ALL*. Thirteen ways to understand the variety of different beings from all Universes and dimensions. You will come to know these archetypes well in future pages.

The Anunnaki had always felt themselves to be rulers higher than the other beings. They were not known for empathy. It was important for the Anunnaki to come to this planet to learn how to be slaves, how to be common people, how to be happy just with what one has.

Entities like the Greys had always been treated as slaves, as though they were the lowest entity in existence. Now on planet Earth the Greys were equal with the Anunnaki and there was no way to tell the difference between them in their human forms. This gave the Greys the opportunity to experience being rulers instead of slaves.

There is so much opportunity on this planet! It was always important that the Terrestrials go back to *ALL* to report what they learned as they progressed through the archetypes. It is not as though people would go back and fill out forms to provide this feedback. The Akashic Records were set up to automatically record everything so *ALL* would know everything immediately.

Each and every human being is a living document of the Great Contract between *ALL* and every type of intergalactic being.

Terra, or Earth, is simply a place for one to learn how to get along with one another. This is where one is to learn how to tolerate and live with each other in Compassion and Consciousness. A piece of *ALL* is in each being and each being has a specific Star Being linage. It is a complex system that can only work because of *ALL*'s greatness.

Humans are all unique. Each is made up in their uniqueness of the same ingredients as the flesh of Mother Earth. The molecules in their bodies are exactly the same molecules that are in space, in the Original Creator Beings, in the very first physical being. These are the building blocks of every cell of one's body.

We truly are *ALL*'s children.

Opportunities Download Experience

Close your eyes and let your mind wander. Feel yourself as Mother Earth. Feel the greatness of you.

Notes

The Second War

As time passed, the more involved different alien guides/deities on this planet began to interfere with human affairs. A few of these Star Beings would still kidnap large groups of Earth beings to eat them or to enslave them. Some of these guide/deity Star Beings mated directly with the Terrestrials, creating new life forms with greater abilities.

The Seraphim began to notice these infractions, knowing it was against The Great Compact. This started a second major war between the Light Beings and the Star Being entities that were trying to remain involved with human lives.

These Star Beings had already snuck in and begun to interbreed, creating different knowledges and different levels of beings and different societies. This was antithetical to The Great Compact, so the Angelic Dragons returned to *ALL*, requesting that all the Star Beings no longer be seen on the planet. It was imperative that the Star Beings stay away. Only this could allow the human race to go forward and create, becoming uninhibited by outside forces and untouched by their soul relatives. This was the balance needed.

ALL agreed with this and demanded that all Star Being guides/deities be removed instantly from the planet. This is when all those whom humans regard as major gods and deities were turned into statues or ascended up into prayer. A few of the Star Beings had already left children on the planet that were considered demigods. These were allowed to stay.

Many ancient myths and stories came from these deities and their different areas, from Shiva and Shakti to Isis and Osiris. Even indigenous people lost their ruling gods when *ALL* banished all Star Being guides and deities.

At this same time, Terra created an underworld – what is also called the Shaman World. This space only exists on Planet Earth. It is not Hell at all; it is the original second dimension deep inside Mother Earth. When The Great Compact arrived, *ALL* put planet Earth into the third dimension to allow it to grow. With this inner underworld, Terra's original state as a second dimension planet found a way to continue to exist.

In the fourth dimension, one's possibilities expand out even further. *ALL*'s Spirits, such as fairies and magic, show up in the fourth dimension.

This second dimensional underworld is the place where one goes down into Terra, deep down into the matter that one is made from. Travel to this Shaman world is about going down into this planet and into this planet's history instead of going up into the Beings of Conscious Light and up into the many Heavens in the Void. The Egyptian Book of the Dead gives the best description of this underworld place, as it is all a part of the complete journey back to *ALL*.

The Second War Download Experience

Close your eyes and let your mind wander. Feel ino the 2nd Dimension. Discover how it feels for you.

Notes

Notes

The doors are open
to all those whose hearts are open to
be part of the Great Awakening

Dimensions

When I speak of dimensions, it is also about adding possibilities. Dimensions are described in linear form by Descartes as taught in basic geometry. The single line (↔) is plotted on a graph or a piece of paper to represent the 1st Dimension. By adding a second line (↕↔), one has increased the possibilities. When that third line gets added (X), now there is X, Y and Z lines or possibilities.

The idea that the mathematician Descartes limits the 1st Dimension to a singular Line is absurd. The First Dimension is the vibrational sound and color expansion of Oneness; a singular line it is *not*. This realm is what one calls the First Dimension. It is the vibration that is held closest to my Dragon head, where Source emanates. It is perfect harmony as one would say. Even what looks to be chaos is so fantastic to be with!

It is a singular Love of Source in brilliant prismatic elevated *everything*. Whole systems of sound, a Love vibration orgy of senses – color, scents, sounds. Think of it as living life at a concert of your favorite band just singing to you live, with scents of your favorite foods surrounding you, and feeling blissfully orgasmic all at the same time.

The 2nd Dimension is not lower or higher than the 1st Dimension, it is simply an expansion of possibilities to the singular Oneness. It is the place where the first Material Life began. It is the Vesica Piscis of the first conscious thought joined with Love. This is not a place where two lines cross, as Descartes would lead one to believe, but a *round* space. It is the space where two wheels cross, the place wherein *ALL* first replicated *ALL*.

The 3rd Dimension happened when the Star Beings got caught tampering with Terra, when *ALL* was shown how the Star Beings (or Aliens as one calls them on Earth) had begun mating and messing with Terra's untouched pure Love. The Star Beings were mating, eating, and redesigning the innocent life forces, as if to push evolution forward faster and faster. Rather than putting a complete stop to this and destroying Terra, *ALL* chose to experience material living on Earth in a new way. Since the Star Beings were now to follow *ALL*'s Will and no Star Being wanted for anything, this entire 3rd Dimension was founded on a curiousness of conscious Love.

The 4th Dimension is alive and well on Earth now. What humans would call natural magic or the mystical can now be felt by all sentient beings. What was once hidden in the shadows is now open and available. What was once considered to be sacred and only to be known by the few is now public knowledge. What was hidden in the shadows is open for all to use with Love. One sees this and feels this in these pages before one.

Planet Earth moved into the 5th Dimension with the tumultuous year 2020. They have sent me, The Dragon Heart, to Terra now so that I may assist with the transition into the 5th dimension. I am part of a physical human person, so here I, too, am limited to the laws of Terra as she expands into this newfound reality.

As of the year 2020, the entire planet has been elevated. The doors are open to all those whose hearts are open to be part of the Great Awakening. In this new era one will find the Fountain of Youth and all healing within one's own body. Possibilities have become unlimited, as now each one *feels* into their future selves.

Dimensions Download Experience

Close your eyes and let your mind wander. Feel into the Dimensions. Allow the information to flow as you feel into each Dimension.

Notes

Notes

Cracks in the Great Compact

If one leaps ahead billions of years, past the twelve separate times that nearly everything on this planet was destroyed for one reason or another, if one looks at the present time...

It was around the turn of the 19th century when the Beings of Conscious Light first became aware that the Great Compact had been broken yet again. Once again, different Star Beings had been coming down to the planet and taking humans off of it for purposes that did not follow *ALL*'s Will.

Some Star Beings were taking the humans as food, some were taking them as slaves. Some were taking them to experiment on, to see if they could get the God spark – to get the soul – out of them and place it into themselves or into other entities. A few spaceships were lost on Terra, never to be reclaimed or to return to their home planet. Many governments and corporations took these spacecrafts and performed reverse engineering to give us our technology that one has today.

It was around the 1930s that a young Sun Soul went missing. This was no ordinary soul; it was a High Princess, a High Priestess from the Mantis people, who were more of a conscious or knowledge-based race. This young Princess had been begging to come to planet Earth with her soul so that she could experience all of life. She wanted to fully understand Compassion so that she could know Love and laughter. The race she came from only understood logic. This Princess/Priestess came to try to save her own race and her own planet. The Mantis People and their world in the Universe had been taken over by other Star Beings many times. Being philosophers had not helped them protect their planet and way of life. To protect their planet, she knew they needed to learn to be not warriors, but farmers.

When the Princess arrived on Earth in her human form, it was everything she had hoped! Her human self had forgotten who she was on Mantis. For her Earth life she had signed up to be just a simple farmer's daughter, but even in her human form, she emanated so much consciousness out of her body so brightly that another Star Being (who was at war against the Mantis) came and took her away when she was in her late teenage years. No one could discover what dimension or place she had been taken to. This was a huge disgrace to the Mantis people, let alone going against what *ALL* had agreed to in The Great Compact.

When the archangels began to look deeper into this situation, they found that two specific Star Being races were consistently breaking The Great Compact. A few other random Star Beings were also breaking the compact, but their reasons were complicated and required no punishment, only redirection. However, there were two full races of Star Beings consistently and purposefully going against *ALL*'s Will. Between the two of them, they were doing enough to Terra to dissolve the compact.

One of these was a star race that was actually taking humans off planet, not to enslave, but to eat. Humans with the perfect DNA were sold as a high delicacy. Another star race was trying to create a third race of humans with no soul star connection, so they would be fully controllable and could be all their very own.

This particular Star Being race of compact breakers was not directly created by *ALL*. They were 10 generations removed from the first Zetas created by the Anunnaki, a hybrid that was diluted with fear. Their connection to *ALL* had been disconnected several generations back. Through science, this star race was trying to reconnect with something they felt they were missing and they thought that creating a new race with humans would supply that missing part.

Descartes was the first human to theorize that the body and mind (soul) could be separated and exist as separate entities. This is what this star race understood as well and they wanted to get the Godspark out of the Terrestrials for their own purposes. They, too, enslaved Terrestrials on some distant planet.

The Mantis Princess was no longer traceable on Earth, but her Godspark – her soul lineage – still existed. The Godspark is unable to be separated from the human avatar. The body, itself, is the contract. She was eventually found through the Cherubim stuck in slavery in the 2nd dimension. Nevertheless, she persisted and learned to be a farmer using no technology, only her wits.

With The Great Compact no longer being honored, the Archangels began to constantly check in on Terra. The planet was in poor shape. She had become weak from years of abuse, being experimented upon, drained, and blown up. Now her temperature was rising. As the human race spread more fear, Terra took the toll. Trees absorbed and transmuted what they could, but it was not nearly enough. The Angels did what they could to repair Terra as the majority of humans on Earth continued to disrespect her and treat her like a disposable life.

Another small issue was also found while researching the loss of the Princess. It was found that some members of the reptilian race were hiding amongst the Terrestrials. The Cetians had discovered a way to cloak themselves in the human form. The Cetians had been created after The Great Compact, so they were left out of the original contract. Still, they figured out a way to participate in life on Terra. This small group became very greedy. To this day they hold much material power on this planet. Most of the Cetians have been removed and the system they exploited has been stopped. Those who are left will be removed from this planet naturally as their human forms complete their life spans.

Cracks in The Great Compact Download Experience

Close your eyes and let your mind wander. Feel this history. See this history. Explore this history.

Notes

A New Compact

In time, Terra began to open up to the Star Beings again, and the Terrestrials summoned the Star Beings to come. In the early 1950's, the Intergalactic Council sent representatives to reach out to governments on Earth. They met with President Truman and other leaders of Earth. Since The Great Compact was broken, they had to act fast before panic set in.

Out in the middle of the California desert, where Giant Rock stood, several Star Beings began communicating directly with humans, working to actively create passageways for distant travel. A Union Ceremony was planned for the grand opening of this star bridge. Unfortunately, the rogue race of Star Beings who had been illegally kidnapping humans from the planet had already infiltrated the government. Before the star bridge could open, it was shut down and all the important travel technology was removed from the premises.

In addition, there was an ambush on the Queen of the Pleiadians who came to Terra for that first Union Ceremony. She had come to be a living acknowledgement of the Star Being lineage contained in the human race. The ambush's show of violence upon the peaceful Pleiadian race demonstrated that the human race was not yet ready for the revelation of the truths that lay within each human being.

Now the Great Compact stands ready to be redesigned. As the Mayan calendar showed in the timelines that *ALL* had set, the human race is entering into a phase of peace and understanding. This phase is also shown in the stars as The Age of Aquarius. It is a time for Love and tolerance to rule.

ALL had already known that The Great Compact would not last forever, *ALL* had written it in the stars, for *ALL* knows *ALL*. *ALL* knew the great chaos of Free Will and fear would have to rule first, setting the stage for Compassion to return. For Compassion *would* return. After all, Compassion created the Archangels, the greatest Love warriors in existence.

As you read these words, this current Now time is the cusp of this expanding era of peace, of this living 5th dimension on Terra.

All on Earth can see that the planet has only just entered into this new time, for the paradigm shifts have begun! Chaos rules Terra for a time as one wages wars, both without and within every individual, but this will fade away quickly. After thousands of years of breeding and different races mating, one would believe that by now we would have created the perfect ultimate being – a balance of the DNA of the Star Beings and the soul light of the Angelic realms. Instead, Free Will gave over control to others and the false perception that God or *ALL* is separate from the individual came to rule.

The start of this new era of peace is the transitional time where chaos and Free Will rules, guided by fear and hate lashing out in one great final burst of effort to remain primary. Thousands of years of control, brainwashing, and hate are instilled into these vehicles, or bodies, even before the Angelic Soul comes in. Although it was hoped that Love would organically rule as it does for the indigenous peoples, it was destiny for Free Will to take over, and when the DNA of the Star Beings got introduced, so did their fear and control methods. It can take some time and effort to unlearn these old patterns and feel comfortable in the Now of peace.

NOW, in this present moment, is the time that we can dream and create our future selves in the most perfect way. Magic is real, Love does conquer all and the more in balance one is with nature and oneself, truly, the easier life is. Live in the Wheel of Life, as the Wheel of Life.

Understanding that *everything* is *ALL*'s Angelic Souls come to life on this planet–that we all come from the same Source–should bring us together even more. The physical differences one sees are directly related to the original Star Beings once represented on Earth through The Great Compact. Through this Great Compact, many of the Star Beings were able to achieve the goal of experiencing all aspects of existence, finding new solutions and discovering new perspectives through their human lifetimes, which have been applied in their own planets and Star races. They have found peace in their Universe. Now it is time for the human race to find peace with itself, for the sake of all lives within human form and all other forms of creation.

A New Compact Download Experience

Close your eyes and let your mind wander. Feel this history. See this history. Explore this history.

Notes

Notes

The Thirteen Archetypes

I believe this to be my last life on Terra as The Dragon Heart. In reading my Akashic Records I understand that I have experienced and completed all of the archetypes we were sent here to Terra to learn and understand. My Soul Star is part of the constellation humans call Scorpio. There are at least twelve other versions of my soul on this planet at any given time. As the doppelganger theory goes, there are other "Dragon Heart Godsparks" out there in 7.53 billion people on Earth, and twelve of us are from the same Soul Star. It is the same for you and your Soul Star.

Each avatar has a different experience through the different DNA that it is made from, but the underlying soul for each is the same. It is simply that each separate avatar is dealing with their own archetype to experience and understand. Who knows? Perhaps all twelve of us are here to elevate mankind at this special time and we will soon be on our way back to oneness. Perhaps we are all experiencing one single archetype and trying to find resolution in twelve different ways; twelve attempts to elevate our planet, or twelve separate pieces to complete one puzzle.

My voice is heard through the avatar called Rachel O. Other avatars hold my scientific knowledge, my unlimited Compassion for the planet. Still others hold space just by being present. One of the gifts of the Age of Aquarius is that one can now choose to come back to Terra just for fun after one's life of experiencing all of the archetypes have been completed!

The thirteen archetypes have been talked about quite a bit in recent history. There are books that go deeper, some even describe specific orders of steps that must be taken for the journey through the archetypes to happen properly and come to completion. While these can be helpful to some, I must point out here and now that there is no one way or right way, nor there is a specific order – we each proceed in our own individual way. At some point all souls need to experience all of these lives.

Because of Free Will we have so many options! One can actually choose to *not* focus on what one's individual purpose is. For example, if one was born into the archetype of an "Everyman" and instead one follows the ego into committing crimes against others, by choice they are not experiencing the "Everyman" archetype. Their soul will be sent back to experience "Everyman" time and again until they complete the understanding of that specific archetype or fulfill their individual purpose.

Here is a simple break down of the thirteen archetypes in no particular order:

- The Everyman/Everywoman
- The Mother/Creator
- The Ruler/Royalty
- The Warrior/Murderer
- The Slave/Victim
- The Civic/Teacher Doctor
- The Artist/Genius
- The Champion/Hero/Heroine
- The Lover/Farmer
- The Conscious/Scientist/Philosopher
- The Spiritual/Religious/Magician
- The Fool/Jester/Innocent

There is also the thirteenth archetype of completion:

- The Whole/Oneness

Intensive studies of the archetypes exist from Carl Jung to New Age Schools for those who wish to delve deeper. Here is an overview of the archetypes as I, The Dragon Heart, have come to know them. Take time to meditate on each archetype to find which one fits one's NOW lifetime.

The Everyman/Everywoman is truly that – it is every person on this planet. It is the unsung heroes from the coal mines to the retail floor. It is the person who can choose to be a victim of a life event that has occurred, or they can step past the mundane and see the joy in everyday life. Lessons learned by the Everyman/Everywoman are that happiness comes from within, and that one is always provided with what one needs. The Everyman/Everywoman can also be a man or woman with or without children who lives simply. This archetype could be considered to be related to the 1st Chakra, Red, for Everyman/Everywoman is a basic, down to earth kind of person. More will come on the chakras in a following chapter.

The Mother/Creator energy is strongly held within the 2nd chakra, the chakra of nurturing and creativity. The Mother/Creator is not limited to being a female mother of children, but also includes males who must learn the nurturing and creation aspects of motherhood as well. The Mother/Creator gives birth to nations, to inventions, to crafting the new in thought and form, but always with a sense of nurturing. With science, technology, and art, the Mother/Creator gives birth to many creations.

The Ruler/Royalty is just what it sounds like, however these are people born to be leaders, not just those born into wealth and lineage. To be a Ruler/Royalty is not about money and gemstones set into crowns, it is an attitude. The statement "Being born to the purple" applies well here, as people in this archetype identify with the color Violet and find their energy at the Crown chakra. Be aware that this archetype does not always represent politicians, as not all politicians were meant to rule. Nor does being in this archetype mean that one will rule for justice and peace. The learning curve can be steep, but ultimately the Ruler/Royalty is an archetype of learning to rule through Love and not control through fear.

The Warrior/Murderer is a broad spectrum as well. The Warrior/Murderer goes from the military person who loves the comfort of following orders, to the human who does not respect life in all its forms. The person who tosses a bag of kittens into a river has not murdered a human but is still committing murder. The Warrior/Murderer archetype goes far deeper than the glamorization of battle and crime in movies. The Warrior/Murderer archetype ranges from the proud United State Marine to teens who plot school shootings. The Warrior/Murderer may be honorably killing, not humans, but an outdated paradigm for a cause greater than themselves. They may be fighting to save lives or to tear down unfair policies. They may be killing for pleasure or sabotaging their own path. There is much range here. The ultimate lesson is to choose Love over fear, judgment-free.

Famous murderers names will live on if fear is to rule. There is a lack of empathy shown for victims in the Warrior/Murderer archetype until the Warrior comes to learn to love their presumed enemy. The energy of this archetype is found in both the 3rd and 4th chakras, as one's self love and heart determine which label one chooses, the powerful identification of the fierce warrior or the destructive power-over-others identification of the Murderer.

The Slave/Victim is a very common archetype that souls tend to repeat again and again before learning the lessons set before them. Although slavery was outlawed in the United States and many other countries, it still is very much present in the world and has many names. From young women and men being trapped into sex slavery to the indentured servants who cut sugar cane fields in Florida to the minimum wage worker who has fallen so far into debt that release seems impossible to the person who has fallen victim to online propaganda and lies. This archetype is alive and well in the modern day.

The Slave/Victim was not my favorite archetype to experience and I have often repeated this lesson over several lifetimes, until now. The lessons of the Slave/Victim archetype are lessons of personal power. Lessons of choice and choosing. Lessons of survival against all odds. Lessons of persistence. Lessons of finding joy wherever joy can be found. Many beings are living through this archetype for the last time. The Age of Aquarius is freeing all beings of Earth from repeating this archetype, as well as any of the other archetypes. This change will happen very quickly for those living outside of time but may take much more time on Earth. The energy of this archetype is mainly found in the 3rd chakra of Self.

The Civic/Teacher Doctor is an archetype that focuses on clearing up messes. They lead with expertise, knowledge and attention to the greater good, finding consensus in divisive or unhealthy situations. In its highest incarnation, the Civic/Teacher Doctor values optimism and teamwork, rebuilding institutions in a heart-centered way. Politicians who take community action, teachers who positively influence and build our future, doctors who relieve suffering. This archetype stands up for the victim or the underdog and keeps our society's morals in check. The lessons of this archetype are to look out for others with strict adherence to a higher truth and to avoid falling into self-service through greed of money or lust for power. The energy of the Civic/Teacher Doctor archetype is strong in the 5th and 4th chakra, as they become very passionate about their work and are great communicators.

The Artist/Genius is often an individualist or a loner category. This is the archetype where one's consciousness is so connected to *ALL*, one often loses one's own Compassion for the physical self. Hours pass like minutes for the Artist/Genius and they are often seen as absentminded or only half here and that is the truth, for they exist in a constant state of inner creation. The world of their imagination has much greater hold on them than the physical world of Earth. They live to create in all forms. The greatest archetype of this would be Da Vinci who was able to find a balance that many artists and geniuses can't find today. Even if art is subjective, this Archetype is not – it is a brilliance that is seen in their daily lives as they express themselves through touch, taste, sound and sight. The energy of the Artist/Genius is the color of the rainbow, of prismatic beauty.

The Champion/Hero/Heroine has many faces. From athlete to war hero the Champion/Hero archetype is far more than a comic book life. A Hero's/Heroine's Journey is a classic storyline that people live every day in creating their individual life story, however it is not one of constant victory. It is an archetype that is filled with challenges to be overcome, either for oneself or for the sake of others. However, unlike the Slave/Victim who is overcome by obstacles that are seemingly beyond their control, this archetype sees adventure in every challenge and has the wherewithal to meet it head on. In times of major crisis heroes and heroines appear with a fire hose, an apron, a face mask, a clip board, a helping hand. As a Champion/Hero/Heroine, one daily takes actions of strength intermingled with pure Love as one's heroic actions. The Champion/Hero/Heroine is of all colors – a balance of oneness for every need.

The Lover/Farmer tends relationships, growing them, evoking emotions, and harvesting their bounty. They look for ways to nurture the world around them as they celebrate the joys of life. The Lover/Farmer is very much attuned to the cycles of the year and the cycles of life. While our first thoughts turn to romantic love, it is important to remember that for The Lover, all forms of Love are included. The love of friends, the love of family, and the love of a Higher Power. It is intimacy and closeness that is important to The Lover/Farmer, whether in the form of a deep and abiding closeness to the people who populate their existence, or as a practical knowledge of animals, plants, seasons, astrology, and weather. The energy of The Lover/Farmer is linked to the green and pink of the Heart Chakra. They are very much aware of the space around them.

The Conscious/Scientist/Philosopher loves thought. Highly imaginative, they live among the possibilities of this and other worlds. Where others see boundaries, the Conscious/Scientist /Philosopher sees the spaces between and beyond. Creative, curious and thoughtful, they look beyond conventional structures. This could be a lonely archetype, but most Conscious/ Scientist/Philosophers are so busy with their own thoughts that they sometimes prefer to work alone. They want to know and understand and they find inspiration in even the smallest of observations. They understand the Universe and communicate this understanding in various ways so others can see the harmony of life's miracles at work. Their energy is seated in the 2nd, 5th and 6th chakras, sacral, throat and third eye, as they intuit new information, test it, and communicate it to others.

The Spiritual/Religious/Magician is the archetype of mystery and transformation. This archetype also dwells in possibilities, but in a different way. They simply *know* things. Beyond that, they transform perceptions and create the future. Intuition plays strongly in this archetype, as does direct connection to the Divine, thus the energies of the 6th and 7th chakras – the energies of the Third Eye Chakra of intuition and the Crown Chakra of peace and wisdom – are intertwined with this archetype. The inner world of Spirit flows to the outer world of manifestation. The Spiritual/Religious/Magician communes with Beings of higher vibration, but is also very much a part of Earth life. They are, in fact, a bridge between the esoteric and the functional. Their communication may come across as cryptic, but it has the unmistakable ring of truth. Others can find the Spiritual/Religious/Magician to be spacey or rather frightening, as they live comfortably in a world that others can't see, but for the most part the otherworldly energy that shimmers around them is an attractant that marks them as special.

The Fool/Jester/Innocent is known to be a happy archetype. They live primarily in a state of acceptance without judgment.

Whether consciously or sub-consciously, The Fool/Jester/Innocent actively embraces and fortifies the innocent parts of themselves to keep themselves pure. For some innocents it can feel as though everyone else got a How To Live A Human Life manual except them. Sensitive, they love constantly, but are easily hurt by the pains of the world. They are also ready to forgive and forget and love again, time after time. The innocent perspective stays with them their whole life. Inner child love rules and they want to be surrounded all the time by happiness and joy and can never understand why the rest of the world isn't on board with this wonderful outlook.

The Fool/Jester/Innocent can seem flighty and erratic as they go in search of one positive experience after another. As they gain a spiritual aspect, the Fool/Jester/Innocent gains balance with the world, becoming focused on gratitude and a search for positive experiences of enlightenment. People in this archetype tend to be aloof. Being linked with others tends to hold them in place and limits their possibilities. Despite the associations that go with the name, the Fool/Jester/ Innocent is uncommonly wise, though their flighty nature can keep the treasure of their wisdom out of sight. Their energy is the pure white of the higher chakras, the pure white light of Oneness.

The Whole/Oneness is the archetype of *ALL*, the final brief step before returning to the eternal embrace of the Creator. Prior to the Age of Aquarius, many miscarriages, still births and children who pass away at a young age have been experiencing this ultimate archetype of full and complete integration. There are others who come to live longer in this archetype of Oneness to share the ultimate in healing and wisdom with Earth and her inhabitants. While the expression of this archetype can take many forms, often people living this archetype live simple lives of contentment and Love, teaching quietly by example and with the silent emanation of their energy. As Wholeness, this archetype includes all of the initial twelve archetypes, as well as having a pathway of Peace, Love, Kindness, and Compassion all its own.

These archetypes have been an important aspect of the lives lived on Earth for millennia. As one enters into the Age of Aquarius one will see these archetypes begin to fade away. The babies being born in the Age of Aquarius no longer have to live each of these lives, for they have already experienced all of *ALL*'s contract! Each and every one of the Soul Stars has experienced all the archetypes. In the Age of Aquarius, the new babies on the planet bring in a true Free Will that is closely aligned with the Oneness of *ALL*. The Oneness with *ALL* is the thirteenth and final archetype, that of living as an Ascended Master on Earth.

The Thirteen Archetypes Download Experience

Close your eyes and let your mind wander. Which of the archetypes has defined your life up to this point? Which archetypes do you believe you have lived in the past? Are you ready to live completely free of past archetypes? What does this look like to you? What does this feel like?

Notes

Notes

Life Lessons of The Dragon Heart

As The Dragon Heart, not only have I experienced all the Archetypes, but I have also been a messenger for many terrestrials. My gifts are unlike many of the famous gods, deities, goddesses, and gurus that you know of, but I have aided many of them. I have been known to serve an apple to expand consciousness. I stood with Moses and honored his words. I worked with many great beings from Lemuria to Tibet. I have held up Quan Yin and worked with all Archangels.

I come from before time existed. I am not of the future; I am in the NOW. I am here to tell the forbidden truths. I am here to be a gateway of Love, to hold the space of Love and open the conscious light to flow unlimited, to allow true freedom of conscious knowledge to flow, just as *ALL* wishes.

It is now time for humanity to understand Love in a new way. It is now time for humanity to come to the acceptance that Love is an energy of unlimited possibilities. This is not a single feeling. It is not limited to touch. Love is so much more than its current description on Earth. Love is judgment-free. Love is precisely what one is made of, simply Love.

This is the essence of my work. I am here on this planet to hold the space of Love. I am here on this planet to release conscious knowledge. Love in practice is the simplest and most complete answer for the world's needs. Now is the time to live heart-centered. Now is Love.

The concept of living heart-centered is for one to live, to think, to breathe through one's own heart. In Egyptian times, the brain or mind was thought to be located in the center of the chest. In Nova Gaia, the thought center is at the fourth chakra. To find the heart chakra on oneself, place one's fingers under both arms, pull one's hands straight from under one's arms into the center of one's body. This is one's heart chakra within one's own body. This is where heart-centered living takes place. Feel it with one's hands and sense it in the space in and around one's physical body.

The Love feeling one has right now exists in all time and space. It will forever be for one's highest good. Let the tingles go through one's body, feel the words as one reads them. It is truly the most brilliant prismatic opalescence feeling. *ALL*'s Love is inside of one at all times and in all places. That is the feeling of how loved one is.

I work for the Holy Mother Mary, the Divine Feminine. I work directly for Love. Love is the great Void. I am here to hold space for Compassion and tolerance. I try to have no judgment. This doesn't always work because in my human form I have forgotten much of who I am and I have yet to learn and remember many layers of my true and complete Being. For Terra still is the learning planet and we are all still learning.

I write as a teacher, I live as a student.

In the year 2020 a major pandemic crisis happened to the planet that had been planned and in the works for 26,000 years. We had been waiting for this time to elevate us in the fulfillment of our spiritual purpose. We, the Beings of Conscious Light, never know the exact plan or how events are supposed to happen. We receive only bits and hints, never the whole. The Universe is like water; it goes with the flow and never stops. Truly, we did not know how the Great Awakening would happen. Life, itself, is a constant creation.

The Beings of Conscious Light know what the opportunities are and they take advantage of these opportunities. This global pandemic of 2020 marked the time for the great connection back to self. We entered into the Age of Aquarius officially as of the New

Moon of February 2021. The final stage of the starting gate of the Age of Aquarius came as the 2020 Winter Solstice anchored in the Age of Aquarius. We have been waiting for this for a very long time and we know what comes of this is going to be amazing, though it will take some time to be fully felt in the human sphere.

Just wait for it. We are all integral to this. We are all doing our part. There are so many transitions that will take place. This Now stage is part of the transition. The Beings of Conscious Light remind every creation that *ALL*, by whatever name you choose to use, has always been a part of one. Nothing can ever separate one from *ALL*. *ALL* is One.

Everything that is for one's highest good will be available with ease and grace. At first, as growth comes, one may not always realize or understand that what is happening is for one's highest interest. There will be pain, loss, and grief. These are healing reactions. With this healing will come great beauty, miracles and moments of wonderment when one can embrace the new paradigm with Love and Compassion.

This is up to each individual. Every one of you that are here listening or reading at any point in time to this message – even if this recording or book is found in 100 years – know this: It is up to us to daydream and to visualize our new future.

Instead of getting caught up in fear and anger, we need to take this time to focus again on Love and Compassion. We will not be living in a dystopian movie world with hoarding and the threat of the end of the world every week. The Four Horsemen of the Apocalypse with all of the addictive imagination of fear is not our future, but we cannot sit by passively. We each have an active role in bringing about the embodiment and expression of Nova Gaia.

Instead of immersing your energy in fear, bring up the high vibrational Love feeling that gives one joyous goosebumps. Once you are immersed in that positive energy, begin dreaming about the future. One holds the key to one's future and the world's future. Why wouldn't one want to dream it as magnificently as possible, staying in this vibration of Love and dance and celebration and fun? That is all that *ALL* has ever wanted from humans with their ego and forgetfulness.

Ourselves have forgotten who One is. That is over and done with in the Age of Aquarius. One is God. One is *ALL*.

It is time for one to dream about one's new future. As The Dragon Heart, I know for a fact that Love is what awaits us. As more and more individuals dream of Love, all visions of fearful futures fade away.

Everyone has the ability to be a true Healer. When an individual heals themself, they heal their personal world. They also create a spark of light that goes forth to heal the entire world. That is what it means to be a conscious person, conscious of one's actions and how they affect others, including the flesh, the feathered, the finned, the many-legged, and the flora.

The 5th Dimension is evolving on planet Earth. Now one has the opportunity to go into higher vibrational living. Each one of you carries the God-Spark. You can Love more and make changes happen in a moment without the ritual, without the symbols of the past, and without calling in any specific deity. This is all possible because one is the Co-Creator.

When one lives a conscious life, it means looking in the mirror and loving who one is in all of your aspects. It means finding one's daily practice or one's daily ritual or whatever makes one feel comfortable and spiritually connected. One needs a daily practice that acknowledges the Divine Masculine, the Divine Feminine, and the great Source, the great Spirit, of *ALL*. Whatever it is one calls *ALL*. It is God. It is Goddess. It is Jesus and Mary. It is Shakti and Shiva, Isis and Osiris – whoever and whatever brings spiritual connection to one.

There is absolutely no wrong way to practice Love and gratitude when one respects all life. There are billions and billions of perspectives. As humans one must learn to stop taking every event so personally and for a moment forgive and imagine what it will feel like to be One again with all of creation. For a moment feel *you* in your entirety.

When one lives a conscious life, one walks in constant joy. This does not mean that bad things don't happen. One gets to walk forward and Love the adventure of life. All sentient beings are in the same chaotic seas, but each has an individual boat. When one person suffers, not just one person is suffering – the whole is suffering. Now is the opportunity to step outside of ourselves. A moment to be fully conscious with nature and one's surroundings.

As the sun rises each day it is a new gift of the present. The only thing I can guarantee is this very moment right now, this present moment that is real. The only thing that truly exists is this time right now and it doesn't matter if one reads these words in two months or ten years. The present moment is the only thing that exists. Take this present moment and enrich it with more Love and Light than one can imagine.

We are all represented on this planet. As you now know, planet Earth is a learning planet. This is where we are learning to get along with the great variety of others in existence. Earth lives in a realm of Free Will.

So many great events have happened because of this planet and the wild card of Free Will. History implies it was random destruction of the Earth that created the Great Compact after the Beings of Conscious Light realized various Star Beings were on Terra playing with genetics and creating not just humans, but satyrs, mermaids and other beings. Instead all such events mark a great segment of existence when *ALL* became directly involved with Earth.

Spirit placed itself into each life on this planet and gave each a consciousness. *ALL* gave the gift of Free Will to do whatever it is one wants to do within the boundaries of Universal Law. One on Earth cannot fully understand Earth's vast and far-reaching history as there are too many varying perspectives.

It does not matter how earthlings started because what matters is the Now. What matters is the understanding that one is here to learn and to Love in a full sense that goes far beyond our notions of romance, but incorporates all aspects of Love for oneself and others.

Now is the time of the 5th Dimension. I am here to help elevate one to that dimension so that one finds what is held deep in one's heart. The system I am currently using to define one's heart space is the chakra system. The chakras are the road map of the spiritual data system of one's physical body. Chakra information is an important tool to use for one's highest good so you can be the Rainbow Being of Life that you are.

Life Lessons of The Dragon Heart Download Experience

Close your eyes and let your mind wander. Are you ready to create a new foundation for Being that is based on Love of the highest order? What does this look like to you? What does this feel like? Is it open to all Beings, bringing Peace and Love to all for ALL? Explore the many beautiful possibilities with an open heart.

Notes

Notes

In the Nova Gaia Love Era, There are Now 13 Major Chakras

Expanded Chakras

One elevates one's personal vibration through one's chakras. Think of chakras as energy discs that are layered upon one another. Chakras hold information on physical, spiritual, emotional and mental issues, both within and outside of one's avatar. There are nine major chakras that are commonly used in modern day times. There are also minor chakras at every joint within the physical body. Chakra energies flow from the center of the body in both directions, front and the back. If the energy of a chakra is blocked, it creates physical issues.

In the Nova Gaia Love era, there are now 13 major chakras which make up the whole Merkaba (light, spirit, body – the energy sphere in which all exists). I am grateful to The Fairie for her work and insights on bringing these new chakras to light and for her powerful writing as co-creator of this chapter. These new higher chakras are not located within the physical but exist within our aura to create a whole 5D system, instead of the outdated 3D. For ease of discovery, however, we will continue to reference body locations in our discussion.

To truly study and know the chakras can take lifetimes, but even a slight knowledge is extremely valuable, as you will find. Here we give you an overview of the layers – or more aptly, the systemic flow – of the Chakra System.

The first chakra we will speak about is the one *below* your feet. **This is the Zero Chakra. It is called the Earth Star Chakra**

Color: Black Seed

Location in Aura: Just below your feet.

Function: Moving us forward, connection to the Earth, taking in Earth energies, connection to *ALL* on Earth.

Many other cultures and peoples have different names for the Earth Star Chakra. It is the foundation for each sentient being on Earth. It is like a birthmark for which plane and dimension one comes from. It is one's mark for being a terrestrial.

The Earth Star Chakra is our portal to connect to the Earth and all the life on it. The Earth Star Chakra is an important and integral part of living in the Nova Gaia energies.

The First Major Chakra is the Root or Base Chakra

Color: Red

Location in Aura: It is the tiny space between one's legs right at the base of one's trunk.

Functions: Grounding, presence, stability of life, how one feels about life.

Does one feel safe?

Does one have a solid, stable base on which to live life?

A perfectly balanced Base Chakra means that we are secure in ourselves and secure in our world. It means we have a solid stage on which we can live, unfold our true existence, dance and thrive. It means our humanity has integrated with our divinity and we feel the freedom to be ourselves in our most joyful expression.

An open, balanced Root Chakra means we are free to switch from survival-based living to thriving, from fight and flight to a balanced alignment. Enjoying life, being fully present in the moment, loving life and living Love, feeling free, connected, and secure. With an open, working Base Chakra comes the feeling of freedom and sovereignty. To be one's own person, with deep roots connecting us to the collective and the Earth.

The Second Major Chakra is the Sacral Chakra

Color: Orange

Location in Aura: Find your 2nd Chakra by placing two fingers below your belly button, then place your palm just under the span of your two fingers. Using one's hands one should feel the energy.

Function: Creation, creativity.

This is where we create all of life, from babies to every other aspect of life.

In the Sacral Chakra we actually translate and manifest every idea and every energy into matter.

Everything begins as an energy, as an idea. As this energy gathers confidence and drive, we manifest it into our reality. The Sacral Chakra is where that creation manifests. It is our life force energy. When this chakra is open, we live life fully, make plans, and create paths to build what we desire.

An open Sacral Chakra in perfect balance is supported by the solid foundation of the Base Chakra, as a stage on which we move and dance with our creation. As an idea is conceived in thought, we give it voice, we give it power. We give it Love and conscious attention. We feel it within our power to create. The energetic path bebecomes solid matter through this chakra as a thought moves through the rainbow portals one by one to end up in the sacral chakra to give it shape and form.

This second chakra holds the key to switching from a survival mindset to a thriving mindset. The switch to all abundance sits here. The Sacral Chakra possesses its own balance. It is sovereign. Life's creation happens from a *knowing* of being sovereign, a creator, in one's own power. One exists in harmony with oneself, fully realized with both the Human and Divine aspects of self.

This is the chakra where we create our own story of physical life on this planet and in this dimension. Lower back pain can be a sign of the Sacral Chakra being blocked. This often happens with money issues and can cause great pain.

Abundance is what one asks for or manifests. True abundance has very little, if anything, to do with money. Beings of Conscious Light do not understand money, as money does not exist outside of Earth. In this Age of Aquarius Earth will join the rest of the Universe in this knowledge and money issues will be become obsolete, a part of our past.

The Third Major Chakra is the Solar Plexus Chakra

Color: Yellow

Location in Aura: It can be found from two fingers above one's belly button to the place where the ribs come together.

Function: Seat of personal power, self-esteem, confidence, respect for self and others.

One's deepest despair and one's brightest brilliance are felt here. This chakra holds all the emotions one feels about one's self.

A fully open Solar Plexus means we trust ourselves as we look at the world with a thinking intelligent heart and a feeling, loving intelligence or mind. We feel safe to create our own lives, honoring all lessons by taking the gift of learning, growing and glowing in all of the gifts that the open upper chakras deliver. A fully functioning solar plexus shines as bright as the sun.

An open Solar Plexus creates the perfect balance of one's own expression and Compassion. In this perfect balance of the Divine and Human, one feels supported, loved and confident. With a balanced Solar Plexus, one is able to listen to one's own discernment, being transparent to oneself and authentic with full integrity.

The Solar Plexus Chakra is the area where one "digests" what others say about one and how one feels about oneself. This is where one feels one's self-esteem. This is where one can easily see and feel one's "dis-ease" within one's self, possibly with heartburn or colitis.

Within the Rainbow Portal or Rainbow Wheel, this chakra holds the final switch that needs to be flipped for true creation to be possible.

The Fourth Major Chakra is the Heart Chakra

Color: Green & Pink

Location in Aura: If you go from under your armpits straight into the middle of your chest, you will find your Heart Chakra.

Function: Center of balance, center of Earth and Spirit, Yin Yang, Divine Masculine, Divine Feminine.

At the Heart Chakra, the past meets the future in this present moment, in this heartbeat.

An open Heart Chakra sees the world with loving, kind, and compassionate eyes. An open heart is able to see what is true and pure. It sees what is of Love and what is not. It sees what creates life and what does not.

An often overlooked part of the Heart Chakra is the Higher Heart Chakra. This is located in the upper chest between the Heart Chakra and the throat area. The Higher Heart is about self-love, applying Love, kindness and Compassion to oneself as much as it is applied to the outside world. In addition to that, the Higher Heart holds all of one's Divine boundaries, the red flags and cautions of that which is not in alignment with oneself. As such it holds self-respect, dignity, and honor.

The Heart Chakra is balanced as it connects our humanity and our Divinity. It connects the Divine Masculine with the Divine Feminine and the past to the future. The heart opens when we feel safe, when we can think clearly and when we have the ability to express ourselves creatively, joyfully, freely.

The Heart Chakra is the beautiful center of all we are. When it is open, it loves. As one loves, it opens. It holds the key to activating all of the Chakras in perfect health as it is itself activated by all other Chakras.

If we have been hurt by others, or if love was used for manipulation in our lives, one may feel a block in this chakra that feels like a sword in one's back.

The Fifth Major Chakra is the Throat Chakra

Color: Blue

Location in Aura: Found from the center of your throat to your ears, its physical expression is the thyroid.

Function: Communication, expressions of one's Truth.

An open Throat Chakra opens up one's ability to express one's truth not only in vocal communication, but also in action. When words and actions match in joyful, free expression, one's Throat Chakra is working. This chakra is supported by a truth toward oneself and the collective based on integrity, authenticity and transparency.

An open Throat Chakra includes the ability to listen and hold space for others, to listen with Compassion, kindness, and Love, without preconceived ideas or judgments.

For the Throat Chakra to be open, we need to feel confident and secure. All of the Chakras on the body below the Throat Chakra need to be in balance and open for the Throat Chakra to find its full freedom in one's brightest and most joyful expressions.

An open Throat Chakra also balances and connects the Heart and Mind to work in unison, so one is speaking from the Heart-Mind and listening through the Heart-Mind.

The Sixth Major Chakra is the Third Eye Chakra

Color: Indigo Purple

Location in Aura: Between and slightly above one's eyebrows.

Function: The Third Eye functions as a receiver of information beyond the physical, it is an open window to all of the Metaphysical senses.

Clairvoyance (clear seeing), Clairaudience (clear hearing), Clairsentience (clear feeling), Claircognizance (clear knowing), Clairtangency (psychic touch) and Clairgustance (clear taste/smell) comes through the Third Eye.

Additional gifts finding their way towards expression through the Third Eye Chakra are Clairempathy (otherwise known as Empaths) and channeling messages from Spirit.

An open Third Eye Chakra sees and perceives beyond the physical senses and trusts in this metaphysical input. It acts as an antenna with which we perceive guidance from our Spirit Guides, including our Angels, our Ancestors, Ascended Masters, and others of a higher vibration.

They are the whispers in one's mind. They are the voices of Love, Compassion and kindness that never scream, that are never mean or angry. They are the voices of guidance and Love.

The Third Eye Chakra is directly connected to the Sacral Chakra. When both are open and work together, one trusts one's creation and one creates trust in oneself and one's world. Together the Third Eye Chakra and the Sacral Chakra form a secondary circle of balance from the center, where the heart resides, and the first circle of balance where we express our truth in freedom and confidence (Throat Chakra/Solar Plexus).

The Third Eye is the first processing station for the incoming universal energy that flows in through an open Crown Chakra. The open heart, confidence, creativity and solid base of healthy and open lower chakras allow for an easier flow of clarity and smoother acceptance of the aforementioned metaphysical gifts of an active and open Third Eye.

The Seventh Major Chakra is the Crown Chakra

Color: Ultra Violet or White

Location in Aura: Just above the crown of your physical head.

Function: Connection to the Universe, thought-will, The Conscious Light Connection.

With a balanced Crown Chakra, one will feel a strong connection to the Divine, a strong spiritual connection to the Universe and everything in it, and be inspired to live a life of meaning, of purpose. When one allows Crown Chakra energy to flow in a conscious way, it forms a connection to the Higher Chakras, the Higher Self and the Cosmic Wisdom.

The Crown Chakra is a gateway to personal growth. To be fully realized, one must integrate Spirituality and the Divine with the Human Body and Mind. As this occurs, it opens the door to connect with the higher Spiritual Chakras

The counterpart of the Earth Star Chakra is the Soul Star Chakra. This is the Eighth Chakra

Color: White Diamond

Location in Aura: About 6 to 8 inches above the head.

Function: Seat of the Soul, Portal to the Higher Dimensions.

As the Earth Star Chakra is your Portal to connect fully to the Earth, the Soul Star Chakra is the Gateway between your immortal "higher" self and the human self. It connects one to a wider picture far beyond the physical Earth plane. It is a path that opens doors to new cosmic ideas, concepts and higher dimensions. The Soul Star Chakra relates to infinite energy, spirituality, supreme divine wisdom and spiritual Compassion. When the Soul Star Chakra is open, one gains access to the Akashic Records. One will remember more about one's true past and gain deeper access to the innate accumulated Divine Wisdom.

With the opening of the Soul Star Chakra we recognize and clear old patterns. This is where we release the last aspects of all that is no longer needed or desired in an expanded Universe. Opening the Soul Star Chakra helps to provide emotional balance and stability. It brings deep inner peace and tranquility.

Access to Divine Wisdom will give you a higher awareness of the Oneness of all that is. When this chakra opens, one discovers more spiritual gifts and learns more about one's Soul Purpose.

The Soul Star Chakra is the first of the Spiritual Chakras – the "higher" chakras – that express themselves in the Nova Gaia Love Energy. These Spiritual Chakras are now activated and freely accessible to every living soul on this Earth. They are the heart and soul of the Maps we are providing as The Cartographers of the New World, guiding humanity forward to a new life and a new way of living in the understanding of *ALL*.

The Ninth Chakra is the Soul Blueprint Chakra

Color: Prismatic White

Location in Aura: About 4 feet above the head.

Function: Soul Blueprint, Center of Knowing, Remembering, Living Christ Consciousness, Contains our Soul Blueprint, our Original Purpose and Life Plan. Full access to the Christ Consciousness, also known as Buddha's Consciousness, Michael's Consciousness.

The Soul Blueprint Chakra opens one up to the totality of one's skills and abilities as learned throughout all of one's lifetimes. When this Chakra opens, we remember and apply the teachings and wisdom from all our existence. The opening of this Chakra marks a time of profound change in one's life on Earth.

The Christ Consciousness begins to integrate inside one's body, mind, and emotions and is lived on the outside. As we remember more of who we are, we recognize and adjust our lives to live our passion, our purpose. All skills we have learned in this and other lifetimes come together so we can fulfill our life's purpose.

A beautifully open Soul Blueprint Chakra makes it easier to connect and communicate with Spirit Guides and Teachers. This Chakra is also known as the Upper Dan Tien, lighting up the Third Eye with golden light. Set in eternity beyond space and time, the Soul Blueprint Chakra "resides at the heart of the Universe, beyond the soul. It is the self that has never been born that will never die" (Stuart Wilde).

With this Chakra open and balanced, one enters the realm of unlimited possibilities. Containing the energy of change and creation, healing occurs on a deep level of being and one gains knowledge, insights, and the recognition that one is perfect as one is. The spiritual body becomes integrated within the physical form.

The Tenth Chakra is the Solar Chakra

Color: Golden Purple Blue

Location in Aura: A dual location 1 to 4 feet both above the head and below the feet.

Function: Transcendent Self.

The Solar Chakra builds on all of the previous chakras and one begins to manifest and put to use many of the skills learned in all previous lives. Whatever one does, one seems to excel at everything. As the barriers between time and space break down, knowledge and wisdom from the ages begins to flow from within.

At this stage one discovers the balance between one's masculine and feminine aspects and all facets of oneself begin to come together in unity from within. When this Solar Chakra opens, one's

DNA is upgraded to bring in deeper healing and we find the ability to live out our dream. Life is full of purpose.

The Solar Chakra has two locations that work together as one. One part extends several feet above the head and the other part goes down the same distance into the Earth. This extends from about one foot to four feet in either direction.

As we connect deeply to *All There Is* within the higher realms, we also root down deeper into the Earth to connect profoundly with the natural Earth energies. This dual connection to nature and the Universe brings the knowing of ourselves as part of the *ALL* and we start living and interacting energetically with the Universe and the Earth in perfect balance.

A constant exchange of information in energy form flows between the two parts of the Solar Chakra. The transfer of energy goes both ways. It is always incoming as much as it is outgoing.

The Solar Chakra is all about completely rooting ourselves in this life, in this Now. It brings the ability to be always present, both physically and metaphysically at the same time. We communicate with energies from within and without, from below and above.

Recognizing the wisdom of all previous experiences, one can look at life and recognize the gifts brought by all experiences. Judgments such as "good" and "bad" become irrelevant and all gifts are welcome.

The Eleventh Chakra is the Sacred Heart or Core Star Chakra

Color: Silver Blueish Radiance

Location in Aura: A dual location that reaches beyond the Solar Chakra.

Function: Advanced Spiritual Gifts.

The Sacred Heart Chakra is where one acquires advanced spiritual skills. One enters the realm of the Higher Self, defined as the Divine Consciousness that unites all aspects of oneself into one. All spiritual knowledge is accessible. When this chakra is open, we fully realize that all challenges are only tools to give us a greater understanding of the self. What once was perceived as personal weakness is now realized as strength. This allows for a deep expansion of personal peace within.

The Sacred Heart Chakra is aligned to the Earth and to water. With this chakra open, one is firmly in the field of thinking and acting globally, universally. Resultant skills may include instant manifestation of thoughts, bi-location - where one is existing in two locations at the same time - and travel beyond time and space. We are unlimited. We feel it and know it, Increasingly, one develops the ability to directly experience this freedom from long held limitations.

Like the Solar Chakra, this Core Star Chakra is bi-directional. It is above the 10th chakra and below the 10th chakra. The distance is no longer important, as it exists beyond limitations.

With the Sacred Heart Chakra fully open, all residual ego is cleared and one can use the power of the mind to transmute thoughts and dreams into matter. Magic and miracles abound when this chakra opens. Communication with other star nations such as Sirius, the Pleiades and Arcturus open up and one begins to find comfort in the vastness of space.

This chakra holds the seat of our Divine Essence. As we go within, we find ourselves existing beyond space and time.

The Twelfth Chakra is called the Divine Gateway Chakra

Color: *ALL*

Location in Aura: The outer reaches of the aura.

Function: The Doorway to the Spirituality of the Cosmos and Beyond, a place where all is Sacred.

The Divine Gateway Chakra is the source of one's strength and power. It opens the ability to create change, not only in the physical dimension but in the nonphysical as well. It is the doorway to the cosmos and beyond.

The Divine Gateway Chakra contains ascension energies. It is the manifestation of the Light Body, propelling one into a new existence beyond time and space.

While the Core Star Chakra contains loving, nurturing, subtle energies that work on the inner worlds, the Divine Gateway Chakra is a vibrant and creative outgoing force. All the advanced metaphysical skills one has accumulated are free to be used in the Divine Gateway Chakra.

Many believe that the Divine Gateway Chakra includes the mastery of the Soul's Purpose within one's human existence. The opening of this higher chakra allows the mundane to transcend into the sacred and mysterious. When this chakra is open it contains enlightenment and communication with the Divine. The Divine Gateway Chakra is the highest of the spiritual chakras. It is the pure link to Source, the Creator, God. We enter the network of the universal energy system of wholeness. We experience and live the accumulation of all dimensions and realities. It links one to a higher consciousness.

The Divine Gateway Chakra is about self-discovery, both personally and cosmically. As the higher chakras open, the Divine Gateway Chakra spirals deeper into the personal, promoting one's spiritual growth, one's spiritual healing, and one's spiritual connection to the *ALL*.

✧

The Thirteenth Chakra is the Unconditional Love Chakra

Color: Morganite pink or emerald green surrounding a rose gold pinkish color

Location in Aura: A dual location arm's length from the body, both in front and in back, slightly below the level of the heart.

Function: Connection to *ALL*, the eternal shining of pure unconditional Love and light.

Experienced in the heart, the Unconditional Love Chakra is connects us to *All That Is*, to Source, to *ALL*. This chakra holds one's eternal Love and light. When it opens, one is always shining bright. The Unconditional Love Chakra connects one to unconditional Love in every single NOW moment of existence.

While other chakras easily fluctuate between open and closed in a human's life until much practice and growth has taken place in order to maintain them in health and openness, the Unconditional Love Chakra is a unique chakra that, once open, always remains open as a gateway.

All previous chakras must be consistently open and balanced for the impact of the Unconditional Love Chakra to come into one's awareness. While there is no shortcut – no way to bypass any of the chakras – the Nova Gaia energies greatly smooth the way for astoundingly rapid progress in reaching this thirteenth chakra.

As a symbol of Love, the rose is often used to reflect this energy of pure unconditional Love. With awareness of the Unconditional Love Chakra comes the realization of unlimited possibilities. One fully brings all collected universal wisdom into daily human life, consistently and constantly expressing this wisdom with unconditional Love.

The Unconditional Love Chakra is present in both the 4th and 5th dimensions. This Unconditional Love Chakra bridges the way from the Spiritual Chakras of the 4th dimension to the higher Universal 5th Dimensional Chakras. Knowledge of these higher Universal 5th Dimensional Chakras is only beginning to emerge on Earth for Terran communication and understanding.

Expanded Chakras Download Experience

Gaze at the following Mandala, created by The Fairie. When you are ready, close your eyes and allow your mind to wander. Feel the colors and the vibrations of the chakras as they shine throughout your Aura. Which chakras wordlessly speak to you? What do their vibrations communicate to you? Explore these feelings and know that so much more awaits you.

Expanded Chakras
https://novagaialove.com/MandalasByTheFairie.htm

Notes

The Rainbow Wheel Meditation

Both as The Dragon Heart and in my current human form, one of my personal favorite spaces to hold is the Rainbow Wheel or Portal. It is the easiest of all the worm holes to use and everyone has access to it at any time, any place, beyond all time and space – known and unknown.

The best way to use this portal is to live a physically and mentally balanced life in your Earth Walk. We have discussed previously how one has the inner Godspark, now we will discuss how to live in balance.

First, feel into the vibration of the sequence of new chakra energies that swirl above one, below one and around one. They all have a beautiful form and meaning. They are the true Divine Feminine and Divine Masculine energies and one will feel them with this meditation. You may go through this meditation by going alternately between reading and being in a meditative state or you may read the entire passage and then fall into meditation, following along as Spirit and the energies of what you have read travel with you.

The Conscious Light is the universal gift, the Nova Gaia Love. The following meditation will show how to take care of one's whole body – keeping one's chakras balanced and keeping oneself aligned and whole.

For this meditation one also calls upon the Source, the God of all gods, the Spirit of *ALL*. This is the Conscious Light, the Compassionate Love, the true energy that flows through all of us. It is *ALL*, the creator of *ALL*.

One needs to come to *ALL* in this meditation as an ignorant and humble human being and humbly ask the Consciousness to guide one into Nova Gaia Love. One must ask that their crown be opened and allow Love to flow through them, imagining this Love expanding out from one's heart. Ask for healing for oneself and for others. Ask for all to receive this Love.

One of the practices shown to my avatar was given to me personally by The Holy Mother Mary. It is recommended to perform this meditation while standing up. If that is not possible, lay down flat on one's back or in one's most comfortable position. This meditation is for each being to make their own daily practice.

We ask that Compassion and understanding flow through all these beings for eternity or until it is no longer necessary in their lives. We humbly say our full names out loud three times.

My name is __________ ___________ __________

Please go ahead and find a relaxed state. If this is being read to you, please close your eyes and relax as the words continue to guide you.

As I am now flying over your head with my dragon body. I would like you to take a deep breath in through the nose. Imagine bringing this breath down into the belly. I want you to feel the power build in your Hara. One's Hara is located two fingers below your belly button, somewhat behind one's Sacral Chakra.

Focus on this energy source as one takes a breath in and slowly exhales out. Feel the energy build in the Hara. Let go of all thoughts. Release completely to the process of connection to self.

As one stands straight and tall, begin to imagine your virtual body or spirit going down to the Center of the Earth. Imagine that one is going down, down, down. Feel one connecting with the Earth. Feel yourself being pulled through the Earth's mantle. Feel oneself going down past the aquifers through the granite, down,

down. As you travel down to the Center of the Earth, see how beautiful Gaia is! Imagine it all as you are guided down to the middle of the Earth.

Om

Let us imagine that the center of Earth is a beating heart of rainbow clear quartz. It is so enormous it feels like the sun, filled with warmth, color, and healing vibrations of light and Love. This is the heart of Mother Earth, this is the heart of Gaia.

Now imagine oneself absorbing strands of her Love vibration. Her Compassion expands to one with hot magma Love. Bring up this hot magma Love and grounding energy to your physical body on Earth's crust. Pull it up, up, through the mantle, up, up, up, through Earth's crust. Continue to imagine this hot magma Love coming up through one's feet.

Say aloud "I invite in Mother Earth's energy."

Feel Mother Earth's hot Love move up one's legs, up, up, up one's thighs, up, up, up.

As one begins to feel Mother Earth coming into one's heart, one also feels her pulling us down as she grounds one. She is holding one strong in the ground like a flagpole. One knows that one is strong with her.

Once we have Mother Earth in our heart, imagine Mother Earth's Love shooting out of one's heart in front and behind one as though one was a "Care Bear™." One is now part of Gaia.

Humbly ask for the Consciousness of the Divine Masculine, Father Sky, to come through your crown. Say or think "I humbly open up my crown. I open up my head to allow the Conscious Light to flow through me." Imagine one's crown allowing this Conscious Light to flow through.

One will begin to feel this Conscious Light pour through one's crown. Feel the conscious ultra violet cool light pour throughout all time and space. Feel how expansively one's Third Eye Chakra is opened. Down, down, down the spine begin to imagine the Chi energy of the Holy Spirit, the Violet Flame or St Germain's Light, gogoing down one's physical body deep into Mother Earth. Down, down, down our legs, allowing The Source to pass through our body and all the way down to Mother Earth's Core. We are healing Mother Earth with this Conscious Light Healing Universal Energy.

Experience the Divine Feminine Love as it goes through one's heart and back up, then out one's crown. We imagine now that we are a conduit with the two energies running through us, one the Divine Feminine, the other the Divine Masculine.

Now imagine these two energies mixing and blending within one's entire being. Feel it as it becomes the true powerful light of who and what you are from deep within your heart. Feel your heart expand across the horizon, past all time and space. This is Nova Gaia Love.

Place one's hands together, leaving space to make a ball of energy. Let the energy itself tell you how far apart to space your hands to the place where one's hands feel natural. Feel the new energy of Mother Earth and Father Sky build up beneath one's belly button. One can imagine the space between one's hands filling with rose gold prismatic healing light.

Next, raise one's beautiful ball of Nova Gaia Love in front of one's heart chakra.

As one holds this ball of Nova Gaia Love, imagine yourself as though you are three inches tall, standing now in between your hands. Imagine yourself standing here in your heart space.

Through your heart, I want you to say out loud three times in your own words "I love you (your name):

I love you _______
I love you _______

I love you _______

Feel the Love of the Universe within you. Continue to imagine oneself within the sphere of Nova Gaia Love as one asks for healing or whatever pressing area of need is in your life.

Examples are: Please take away my fear of _____. Please allow me to no longer worry about a situation. Please help a physical need like stomach aches, headaches, or mending bones. Bring in abundance - whatever one's concerns are now.

Say it or think it into one's own perfect bubble of Nova Gaia Love. Visualize oneself healing, visualize oneself in the most perfect state of Love. See yourself as your higher self in its most perfect form, for God loves you. *ALL* loves you. Just exactly the way you are. You are perfect.

After one has spent a few moments on oneself, seeing one as strengthening healing Love, next place one's partner or family or closest loved ones in the bubble of Nova Gaia Love you have created. Those who you worry about, even though you're not supposed to worry. Put them in your bubble, then imagine yourself there with your family. Imagine yourself there with your partner or loved ones and say out loud three times:

I love us.
I love us.
I love us

Feel the Nova Gaia Love energy flow through your heart. If the people in your bubble have physical needs, if you have concerns for them of any kind, give it now to the bubble. Tell the Nova Gaia Love what healing needs to be done.

Ask for the highest good to come to all and for *ALL*

Expand one's Nova Gaia Love bubble out to include one's home, then the people with whom one works, then expand it out further to where one lives, past one's country.

Expand this area to completion in the now with the world. Imagine planet Earth between one's hands. Send beautiful blue emerald green Love to this planet, for we are existing in the time of living through the prismatic rainbow of Love.

Once again, say out loud three times:

I love *ALL*
I love *ALL*
I love *ALL*

Send that healing light to the entire planet, including every fish and every insect and every animal. Send Love to the water, the rocks, the food we eat. Allow them to feel the Love and the Light. The more we do this, the more conscious light we bring in.

After one loves the planet and one has sent out Love, bring your rose gold prismatic ball of Love and Conscious Light above your head and open up your ball of Nova Gaia Love to surround you by sweeping your arms out and to the side.

This ball is not a protection bubble, for there is nothing that one needs to be protected from. It is a bubble of Light and Love that will continue to heal one, that will continue to hold one in comfort with *ALL*'s Will.

In the end as you pull yourself back into your body totally and completely, open your eyes and give thanks to Mother Earth and bow to Father Sky.

This is the simplest way to do a daily practice to send healing energy to yourself and to your family. It is this Conscious Light, this wisdom, this knowledge that now goes into us. It is refreshing, taking one beyond hope to healing. It is the understanding that we have already succeeded, that we do not fail at anything.

For a moment each day, feel this Conscious Light. Be a part of *ALL* Consciousness as this Light and Nova Gaia Love energy flows through one. You Are a Being of Conscious Life.

This universal gift does take up to a 14-day period of adjustment within oneself. One may feel fuzzy headed or tired, not from being sick, but from changes taking place deep within. A hint of this fuzziness may never completely go away because, for the present, this is part of the energy of living Now in The Universal Fifth Dimension. You will adapt and find it to feel less fuzzy in time.

Healing reactions may also happen in this time. This may manifest itself as not being able to sleep, hearing a buzzing sound, either binge eating or not eating at all. Physical pains may also appear where one might store past hurt feelings or trauma that has not yet been not dealt with.

Be kind to yourself during this period of adjustment. Listen to the birds, go watch the sunset, experience nature in all parts of this Love experiment. Become the Rainbow Wheel in your daily life. Feel the balance of you and the Godspark as the colors of the Rainbow Wheel keep you moving forward in Love.

Be sure to take time for yourself and your self-care. Be kind to yourself and your body. Find the balance of the rainbow light body that is unique to you. Allow Love to rule through one's heart and find a daily meditation or practice, be it the one presented here or another, to help guide one's heart back to Source.

The Rainbow Wheel Meditation Experience

As you listen to your own guidance, sink into the Rainbow Wheel Meditation to hear, see, and feel Nova Gaia Love and to send it to others. What do you see? How does this feel?

Notes

A Final Word From The Dragon Heart in Her Human Form.

This is truly the time of all times to be on Earth! All becomes stronger as each and every individual works to expand the consciousness of *ALL*.

We need to be strong within the Earth *Now*. We are here in the present to be strong in our Light. It is only going to be more awesome tomorrow – focus on your happiness and what fills you with joy! One is only limited by one's own imagination for what one can create and how one lives.

Understand that you already exist in the 5th dimension, a place beyond limits. This Universal Gift is a way of living, not just a weekend pass. It is about changing the way one feels. The actions one takes is part of *ALL* and everything around one is part of the energy of Love.

You, the individual reading this now, it is up to you to find your walk. Find a meditation or a prayer. Walk alone in nature, find a practice like yoga or Tai Chi – any activity that will help keep your chakras balanced. You need to make yourself happy, for after all that is what your Earth Walk is designed for.

Life is the experience of Love. Let this meaning of life rule one's being – your purpose of experiencing Love.

I Love you all so much.

Thank you so much for *Being*.

A Final Word from the Dragon Heart Meditation Experience

Place your hands on your heart and feel the Love that emanates from you. Recognize that others around the world are doing this as well. Feel that Love move around and through you. Send and receive Love.

Notes

A Final Note from The Cartographers of the New World

And so we come to the end of our Map of Prophecy. Through the downloads in this book you have been given the power to create your own path, the power to forge ahead in your own way. Look back over the notes you made as you traversed this map. See and feel your growth. Your future is yours. It will bring you closer to rejoining *ALL*.

While many people are surprised by the changes of Nova Gaia and may have difficulties in accepting that the world is moving in a different direction, it is all part of the unfolding of the Age of Aquarius where humanity, unity, and community take center stage.

In this new era of Nova Gaia energy each individual is their own authority, their own guru, their own leader. We exist in a community of respect and Compassion and Love. Ego is no longer the driving force among humankind. Here we celebrate and encourage ourselves and each other with a whole heart and a conscious mind. Here we are co-creators of the World's journey.

We are grateful to you for taking this map and forging your own path. We are grateful to you for accepting the responsibility of leadership for yourself while respecting the self-leadership of others. You are a beautiful part of a wonderful whole. Welcome to this part of the journey.

We hope to cross your path again in our forthcoming Heroic Map of Nova Gaia. This next map will lead you to a special place where you will discover the hero, the heroine, that you are and always have been.

What You Do for Others,
You Do for Yourself.

The Cartographers of the New World:

The Dragon Heart is Rachel Otto
The Fairie is Gitte Europa
The Angel is Kay Adkins

novagaialove.com

Made in the USA
Columbia, SC
18 April 2021